Jim Cliff

STARTING A PODCAST IN 2020

Jim Cliff

Also by Jim Cliff

Fallacious Trump: The Donald J. Trump Guide to Logical Fallacies
The Best Words: The Collected Wisdom of Donald J. Trump
The Ultimate, Unofficial Friends Quiz Book
The Ultimate USTV Quiz Book: The '80s
The Ultimate USTV Quiz Book: The '90s
The Shoulders of Giants: A Jake Abraham Mystery
Bad Memory: A Jake Abraham Mystery Novella

STARTING A PODCAST IN 2020

Copyright © 2020 Jim Cliff

ISBN: 9798650816041

Published by Antbear Books, 2020

Ipswich, UK

All rights reserved. No parts of this publication may be reproduced, stored in a retrieval system, or transmitted in any form or by any means, electronic, mechanical, photocopying, recording, or otherwise, without the prior written permission of the copyright owner.

This book is sold subject to the condition that it shall not, by way of trade or otherwise, be lent, resold, hired out, or otherwise circulated without the publisher's prior consent in any form of binding or cover other than that in which it is published and without a similar condition including this condition being imposed on the subsequent purchaser. Under no circumstances may any part of this book be photocopied for resale.

About the Author

Jim Cliff appeared on his first podcast in 2007 and has been slightly obsessed with the medium ever since. Now a full-time video & audio producer and podcast consultant, he has worked on podcasts for various businesses, from one-man companies to large financial institutions. He produces and co-hosts the popular politics and critical thinking podcast, *Fallacious Trump*, and regularly guests on other shows in a number of different genres.

If you need some advice, podcast consultation, or just to let him know how your new podcast is going, you can contact him at jim@jimcliff.co.uk

Jim Cliff

Contents

About the Author...3
   Introduction..9
1. Creating your show...10
   Choosing a topic..10
   Will enough people want to listen?...13
   Hosts and guests...14
   Format and structure...20
   Frequency and duration...23
   Choosing a name..27
   Choosing a podcast media host..30
2. Equipment...33
   Microphones and audio interfaces...33
   Headphones...38
   Mic stands and boom arms...39
   Pop filters..41
   Sound treatment..42
   Field recording..44
3. Pre-production..45
   Should I just make it up as I go along?....................................45
   Intros...48
   Music and stings...50
   Playing music or audio clips...52
   Outro..55

How to interview people.. 56
How to find guests.. 59
4. Production 62
   DAWs (Digital Audio Workstations)........................... 62
   Remote recording.. 67
   Minimizing ambient noise.. 70
   Mic technique... 72
5. Post Production 74
   Editing... 74
   Bitrates and LUFS... 76
   Auphonic.. 79
   ID3 tags 81
   Show notes 83
   Transcripts.. 85
   Audiograms 88
   Outsourcing 90
6. Distribution 92
   RSS feeds 92
   Podcast Mirror... 94
   Submitting to iTunes/Apple Podcasts....................... 96
   Cover art... 98
   Distribution to podcast apps & directories 100
   YouTube.. 103
   Analytics 106
7. Marketing.. 109
   The launch.. 109
   Your website.. 111
   Social media.. 113

Merchandise	115
Cross promotion	116
Press	117
Advertising	118
8. Monetisation	120
Patreon	120
Affiliates	122
Sponsorship	123
Picture Credits	125
Index	126

Jim Cliff

Starting a Podcast in 2020

Introduction

People start podcasts for all kinds of reasons. I don't know what your reason is, but whether you're looking to grow your personal brand; market your business; or just enjoy a fun new hobby, I'm pretty sure the tips in this book will make the whole process a lot easier for you.

You could figure out everything here yourself with a bit of effort, a lot of time, and a few mistakes along the way, but I've been through it myself, and as a podcast consultant I've helped several clients launch podcasts of their own.

Since you're new to podcasting, most of the options I'll recommend will be on the lower end of the budget range, with free options where possible. Sure, you *can* spend a lot of money on microphones, and there are some expensive media hosts and recording software options that probably have loads of great features, but why not start small and then invest more as you get more successful – or just more obsessed with podcasting!

I like using examples to explain things, so I'll be talking about all different kinds of podcasts – some may be more relevant to the kind of show you want to make than others, but bear with me. One example I'll mention quite a lot is the main podcast I co-host, *Fallacious Trump* – I do, after all, know it quite well. Let me quickly explain the concept here so that it makes sense later. Each episode we look at a different logical fallacy, and illustrate it with examples from US and British politicians and popular culture. Along the way we talk about critical thinking and politics as well as current events.

You ready? Let's get started!

1. Creating your show

Choosing a topic

Since you've bought a book on podcasting, I'm guessing that you already have an idea for a podcast. But if you don't, or if you're trying to decide which of your many ideas to go with, here are some things to think about.

The most important thing is that you have to make sure the topic you pick is one that you're really, really interested in, and can talk about for a long time. Depending on some things we'll decide later, this might be a topic you keep coming back to every week for maybe years to come.

Even if it's something you're fascinated by, is there enough in the topic to sustain a podcast for a long time? For example, let's say you really like the TV show *Firefly* and want to do a rewatch podcast? Once you have discussed each of the fourteen episodes and maybe spent a couple of weeks on the movie *Serenity*, will there be anything left to talk about?

Maybe longevity isn't important to you, and you're happy making fifteen or sixteen episodes and calling it a day? That's fine, if that's what you want, but you may find you get bitten by the podcasting bug and don't want to stop. Also, it can take time to build up an audience, so such a short run may make it harder to find listeners.

Of course, any subject can be expanded with a little imagination. With our *Firefly* example, maybe you could go through the whole

Starting a Podcast in 2020

series focusing just on Captain Reynolds, then start all over again with another character. You see?

Apart from expanding the scope of your subject, finding an interesting or quirky way to approach your topic can also help you stand out among other podcasts. This becomes even more important if you choose a really common or popular topic.

What if you wanted to do a show where you interview entrepreneurs or start-up owners about their businesses, how they got started, and what advice they could give to people just starting out?

Well, there are lots of people who would want to listen to a show like that, and there's no shortage of entrepreneurs who would be happy to be on your show. That's why shows like *Entrepreneur on Fire*, *How I Built This* and *The Tim Ferris Show* are so huge. It's also why there are literally thousands of shows trying to compete in that genre.

I'm not saying you can't break through the competition. But to have a chance of standing out, especially when some of those shows have been going for years and have well established audiences, you're going to have to try that much harder to come up with a new angle. You're going to need to make it interesting to people in a way that they haven't heard before, or in a way that not very many people are doing.

The great thing is that you are unique. You're the only version of you. So how you approach a subject will probably be different to how anyone else would approach it. But it's not enough just to say *"well, I'm me. And no one else approaches this subject like I do"*. You have to be able to sell that to get people to listen

11

So, find a topic you're interested in, and then find a way of looking at it which is a bit different.

Will enough people want to listen?

Job one in answering this question is figuring out what 'enough' means to you. More 'mainstream' shows might have a bigger potential audience, but a lot more competition. More 'niche' shows may not appeal to as many people, but I guarantee there are others out there who share your interests, and if your podcast is easy to find and well produced, you'll find an audience.

How big does that audience need to be for you feel like it's worth making your show? If you're hoping Fortune 500 companies are going to advertise on your stock tips podcast, you'll need well over 20,000 U.S. downloads per episode. However, if your podcast is designed to bring customers into your bakery in rural Minnesota, then you don't need the large numbers, just a loyal and hungry local audience.

With *Fallacious Trump*, two years in, we get anywhere from 1,200 to 1,800 downloads per episode. We're certainly not going to make a living from it, but then we're really just doing it for fun. If you told me that I could stand on a stage and that many people would give up an hour of their time every couple of weeks just to hear what I had to say, I'd be pretty amazed. Even if we still only had a few hundred listeners I'd keep doing it, because I love what we do.

Hosts and guests

Once you've decided what your podcast is about, the next thing to think about is who is actually going to be on the show. Will it just be you? Will you work with a co-host – or multiple co-hosts? Will you have guests on some or all your episodes?

These three options can cover pretty much any kind of podcast. Whether you're talking about the latest video games or creating an audio drama set on a pirate ship, you can make it a one-person show, work with a regular 'cast' or invite new people on each show.

Each option has its own advantages and disadvantages – there's no right or wrong answer, and there are many successful examples of each kind of show. If you're having trouble deciding, think about the podcasts you like to listen to. What do you like about them?

Solo podcasts

Advantages:

- You have complete control.
- You can record whenever you want – you don't have to schedule it with anyone else.
- You get to decide exactly what the podcast is about; the tone and content is all yours.
- No danger of having to skip a week or change your format because a guest backs out or your co-host is ill.
- If you decide your podcast has run its course and you want to stop, you're free to make that call.

- This is by far the simplest and cheapest setup in terms of tech and software.

Disadvantages:

- There's nobody to share the work. Unless you outsource, it's all on you.
- You are solely responsible for coming up with ideas for episodes and all the research.
- With just one voice, it can be harder to keep it interesting and keep your energy levels up.
- You have to be very self-motivated to record and edit consistently.

A lot of solo podcasters write a script for their themselves, so they tend to be less conversational in tone and more often educational or informative. That said, if you're really passionate about your subject that can definitely come across.

Co-hosts

Advantages

- More than one person to share all the work and come up with ideas.
- Multiple points of view mean it's more likely listeners will relate to what's being said.
- Podcasts with co-hosts can sound a lot more like a conversation and often feel more relaxed.
- Different hosts might have different backgrounds or areas of expertise they can talk about intelligently.
- With someone else to be accountable to, it can be easier to keep the high level of motivation needed for consistent podcasting.
- Many listeners will keep on listening purely because they enjoy the chemistry between the hosts.

Disadvantages

- It's a much more complicated setup. Whether you're recording in the same room or remotely, you need more equipment and there will be a lot more troubleshooting to get everything working OK.
- The edit *will* take longer. With co-hosts you're more likely to go off on tangents, and there'll be more points where everyone's talking at once.
- You don't control what the other people say! How well you cope with that depends on how much of a control freak you are.
- If you want to change something about the show, it's not just your call. You may have some persuading to do, and at times you'll have to compromise.

The accountability point is important. Some of us are natural procrastinators, and if it's just you that's involved and you don't feel like recording on the day you'd planned to record, what does it matter? That is a quick route to pod fading. However, if you know you co-host has done all their prep and is expecting you to be online at 7pm, you probably won't want to let them down.

On the other hand, if you're one of those people with amazing self-control, will power and determination, that's great – you'll be able to keep a show going by yourself (although you should know, the rest of us don't like you, but it's mostly because we're jealous).

If you decide to go down this route, choose your co-host(s) carefully.

If the show goes well and you enjoy making it, this is someone who you're going to be talking with on and off the air a great deal, possibly for years. You want to make sure that the person that you're talking to is someone that you get on with really well. Someone that you share similar interests with, similar goals, and a similar sense of humour.

Starting a Podcast in 2020

Will you be able to rely on that person to do their share of the work? Can you disagree about things and still stay friends? Will they fairly evaluate your ideas and volunteer ideas of their own? Have a conversation before you start about what they're hoping to get out of this adventure. If they have dollar signs in their eyes and you're just looking for a fun hobby, it's important to know that early on.

If your podcast is successful and then something happens that means your co-host wants to leave, replacing them might not be possible without fundamentally changing the nature of your show.

Of course, nobody can know what will happen in the future, but thinking about some of this stuff in advance can reduce the chances of having trouble later.

Shows with multiple co-hosts can deal with the loss of one more easily – the *Skeptics With A K* podcast from the Merseyside Skeptics Society lost one of their three hosts after five years, and have gone from strength to strength ever since after a new host joined.

The right co-host can make a podcast infinitely more enjoyable, both for the listeners and the podcasters. Personally, many of my favourite podcasts have more than one host, and I don't think *Fallacious Trump* would exist at all if I didn't enjoy chatting to my co-host Mark as much as I do.

To enjoy the benefits of a co-host while avoiding some of the difficulties, I recommend having one person who is kind of 'in charge' of the podcast, like an anchor in a news broadcast, even if there are multiple hosts.

Interview shows

Interview shows can work with either solo hosts or multiple co-hosts, and the interview can be the entire show or just a segment in a longer show – even an occasional segment.

Advantages:

- Your guest will provide a lot of the content – you just have to guide the conversation.
- With different guests each time, your podcast content will be a lot more varied.
- Great way to find more listeners – if your guests already have an audience and they promote their appearance on your show then new people will listen.
- Opportunity for you to talk to interesting people – maybe influencers in your industry who you might not have the chance to meet otherwise.
- You don't have to be the expert on each subject your listeners are interested in – your guests can provide the expertise.

Disadvantages:

- If your podcast relies on interviewing guests, you have to find new guests to interview all the time.
- Scheduling your recording session can be a lot more complicated.
- Guests can let you down at the last minute, leaving you without a show.
- There are a LOT of interview shows. It can be very hard to stand out.
- Being a good interviewer is a skill that you may need to learn.

While your guest will provide the content and the expertise, that doesn't mean there's no work for you to do. There's often a lot of research involved before you interview someone, firstly to let them know that you have taken the trouble to find out a little bit about them and secondly to be able to ask them the kind of questions that will result in a good interview.

There are lots of ways to find guests, which we'll talk about in later chapters, but the kind of guests you can expect to get, and the ease with which you'll find them, depends on your niche. If your podcast is about astrophysics you might have a harder time than a podcast about old TV shows.

Scheduling is the other main headache with guests. Especially when you're just starting out, you are often asking them to essentially do you a favour. They may get some benefit from doing it as well, but if you're a beginner podcaster, then you're definitely not able to say to them, *"Hey, I'd really like to have you on my podcast, but I can only do 12.30 next Tuesday"*. Ultimately, you're going to have to work around them. An interview podcast is easier if you have a lot of flexibility in your schedule.

The fact that interview podcasts are so popular can be a blessing and a curse. Yes, it's harder to stand out, especially if your topic is a popular one, but that can also give you a good way to find new guests. You can listen to other shows in your subject area and contact the guests you find interesting – they're obviously amenable to appearing on podcasts. And if the hosts of those shows are experts themselves, they are also likely to be interested in appearing on other podcasts to find new listeners for their shows – podcast hosts make great guests! In Chapter 3 we'll talk more about where to find guests for your interview show.

Format and structure

The format that your show takes will to some extent be dictated by the topic that you pick, and the kind of show you have. If you have an interview show for example, then at least part of your show will be that interview.

It may be that the interview is your entire show, and you start by introducing your guest, then you do the interview. Then at the end, you thank them for being on the show and give your listeners a call to action to find out more about your guest.

If you're doing a podcast about a current TV show where two or more hosts are talking about the latest episode, again it may be that you have a very stripped-down format that just has a quick introduction, the meat of the podcast, and then the outro.

And that's fine if that's what you want, but there are other options. Maybe the hosts talk for a brief time about the episode, then you have an interview with someone, then you talk about recent news about the actors or some behind-the-scenes information. There are as many different ways to approach each subject as there are podcasts.

Think about it like a magazine-show, like *Good Morning America* or, if you're in the UK, like *This Morning*. They'll have news items, interviews, more in-depth discussions and something more light-hearted. You can use this kind of model to create different segments for your podcast.

Before you record your first episode, brainstorm some ideas for different segments, especially if you have a co-host. Think again about podcasts you enjoy listening to and what you like about them, and talk together about different ideas you think might work for you.

One thing that might be good to think about is introducing some interactivity into your podcast — a question your listeners can answer, listener suggestions for topics or guests, or taking questions from the audience by email or social media that you can answer on the podcast. Giving people an opportunity to feel like they are part of the show can create a more engaged and enthusiastic audience. If you choose to do this, don't worry about not getting much feedback at first — it can take a while to build a community.

I'm a strong advocate of doing at least one practice episode so that you can start to get comfortable with the content and see how things work. Once you've recorded and edited an episode you might choose to revisit and adjust your format before recording your first real episode.

The main thing about the format that you need to be thinking about before you start recording your show is that it's great to be consistent. If you have the same format all of the time, or at least a similar format, then people will get used to listening and there'll be parts that they like, and maybe there'll be parts they don't like as much but they'll know that there's another bit coming up that they usually enjoy. So, if you have a regular format that you stick to, it can help you engender a better and more loyal listener base.

It's also a good idea to make sure you have a beginning, a middle, and an end, even if your format is very basic.

Your opening serves not only to introduce the host(s), but also to talk about what the podcast is all about, in case it's the first time that someone's ever listened. It will also give people an idea of what to expect and why they should keep listening.

Then the middle section, the 'meat' of your podcast is the interview, or the main topic that you're going to talk about, perhaps with your co-host or your guest. Again, this may be split up into several different sections.

Finally, an outro might give people information about how to find you on social media or where to go to find out more about your guest, or it can be an opportunity to ask your listeners for feedback. Either way, it winds up the episode neatly.

Frequency and duration

A couple of very common questions that people ask when they are just starting out with podcasting are *"How long should my podcast be?"* and *"How frequently should I make a new episode?"*

A common answer when you ask the duration question online is between twenty and forty-five minutes because that's the average commute in the US, and therefore people will listen to your podcast on their commute.

If you want to go with that as advice, then go ahead. Personally, that isn't how I consume podcasts. Sure, I do listen on my commute, but I also listen while shopping, cooking or going for a walk in my lunch hour. Other people listen at the gym, while walking the dog, or doing the housework.

I listen to a lot of podcasts, and I don't choose them because they fit into some predetermined time slot. I choose them because they're interesting or funny or I like the hosts. If I'm listening in the car and I get to work before the episode is finished, then I listen to the rest on the way home.

So, I don't think the average commute should determine how long your podcast is. I think a much better question is *"How long will it take you to say what you want to say?"*

Apart from consulting on podcasts, my day job is making videos. People on YouTube have a notoriously short attention span, and my clients often ask me how long their videos should be. I tell them *"As long as it needs to be, and no longer"*.

I'm not being snarky when I say that (well, not much). My point is that you shouldn't waste people's time or outstay your welcome, but different subjects require different amounts of time. A promo for a new flavour of soft drink probably doesn't need more than thirty seconds, but an instructional video that shows you how to put your trampoline together might need ten minutes.

It's the same with podcasts. How deep into your subject do you want to go? How much detail do you think your audience will find interesting? If you're doing a weekly podcast about new restaurants opening up in New York City, maybe a fifteen to twenty minute show is enough, but if your podcast is about existentialism and the meaning of life, you might need longer to really get into the subject.

Consistency is worth pursuing in this - if you are making episodes which are fifteen minutes long, then you probably don't want to suddenly have an episode in there which is one hour long, and the same in the other direction.

However, that doesn't mean that you have to choose a duration before you start and stick to it forever. Especially as you build up an audience who are loyal to you, and who are interested in what you have to say, you may end up talking about more stuff or talking about the same stuff in more detail, and your episodes may stretch. When we started out on *Fallacious Trump*, our episodes were roughly forty-five minutes each. Two years in and now they're consistently over an hour, and no one's ever complained that the episodes are too long.

Another crucial question, is *"What is achievable for you?"*

Let's say you want to talk about Civil War battles, and the level of detail you want to go into would make each episode two to three hours long. You may be a fascinating and knowledgeable speaker who can hold your audience's attention for that long. The amount of work and time required to prepare, record and then edit such a lot of audio will be huge. The show might be amazing and educational, but is that something you can sustain long-term?

Starting a Podcast in 2020

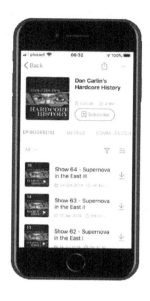

It's not impossible, of course. Dan Carlin's show *Hardcore History* can last up to six hours per episode. But then Dan only releases two episodes per year. His last three episodes have been part of a series on the Asia-Pacific War. The series started in July 2018 and listeners will probably have to wait until late 2020 to hear the end. Dan's probably a bit of an outlier.

The relationship between duration and frequency is in important one. You would probably find it hard to produce a two hour show every week even if your subject is a straightforward one, unless it's your full-time job. In practice, the more frequent your episodes are, the shorter they are likely to be.

Say you wanted to put out a daily podcast giving your perspective on the day's news. Making your episodes an hour long not only requires an extreme amount of your time, but it's also asking a lot of your listeners. Few people can give up that amount of time unless yours is the only podcast they listen to. And if they go on holiday for a week, they may never catch up. However, if your daily show is ten minutes long, then that's really achievable for you and for them.

If your show is once a week, then half an hour or forty-five minutes is not too difficult. If your podcast needs to be an hour and a half or two hours, then maybe it would be better for everybody to only put an episode out every other week, thereby giving you plenty of time to prepare and produce and edit the show, and not overwhelming your listeners with too much audio.

Of course, the subject of your show might have an impact on how frequently you release an episode.

If you are talking about a current TV program then you'll probably want to put your podcast out every week, after the program has aired. On the other hand, if you're talking about the Kings and Queens of England, then it doesn't really matter how frequently your podcast comes out, or how long it is.

Starting a Podcast in 2020

Choosing a name

There's a lot of factors to consider when choosing a name for your podcast.

When people first encounter your podcast in their podcast app, the name is one of only two things they'll see. The other is your cover art. Getting them to click to see more — to find out if they want to give you some of their valuable time — is your goal in choosing a name.

Ideally you want a balance between intrigue and clarity. If you have a quirky, interesting name that doesn't tell people what your podcast is about, then your cover art has to do all the work, and when people just see or hear the name, they'll likely be confused.

A good test for whether your chosen name is too obscure is to ask someone *"If you heard about a podcast called* [your podcast name here], *what would you think it was about?"* If they can guess it within a couple of tries it might work. If they tell you it sounds interesting, you might have your first listener!

For example — if I told you I was thinking about making a podcast called *The Trolley Problem* what would you think it's about. Maybe philosophy? Ethics? Even if you knew it was in the TV section of Apple Podcasts you might not guess that *The Trolley Problem* happens to be one of my favourite episodes of the NBC show *The Good Place*. That's right, it's a *Good Place* rewatch podcast! (It's not, I made it up)

I might struggle to produce cover art that makes it really obvious without infringing NBC's copyright, but you wouldn't have to be *such* a big fan to guess the topics of real Good Place rewatch podcasts *Forking Bullshirt*, *Everything is Fine* or *The Medium Place*.

All of which are much more interesting names than NBC's official one: *The Good Place – The Podcast.*

It used to be the case that you could add an explanatory part to the show title to make a quirky title clearer. If I could get away with *The Trolley Problem – A Good Place Rewatch Podcast,* then I wouldn't have anything to worry about. But in 2020, Apple are being a lot stricter about the names they accept, and any hint of keyword stuffing can get your podcast rejected before you even start.

The rules aren't very explicit, but the word is that people have had trouble with even this kind of clarifying phrase, so it's probably better not to rely on that when coming up with a name. While we're at it, Apple will also reject your podcast if the name includes any expletives.

Probably one of the most important factors is finding a name that is unique. When people search for the name of your podcast online, you want to be easily findable. If you try to put out a podcast with a name of a podcast that already exists, or if you try to use an existing brand name, or the name of a popular book or movie, you'll probably run into difficulty.

So, the first thing to do when you think you have a good name for your podcast is to Google the name and see what comes up. Then add 'podcast' to your Google search and also search in iTunes (Apple keep talking about rebranding it to 'Apple Podcasts', but the transition isn't complete yet). If you get a hit, even if it's a defunct or obsolete podcast, you may want to rethink because it might get confusing for people.

You'll want to avoid using common terms, as well. For example, if I wanted to call my *Good Place* podcast *Janet* after my favourite character, there's very little chance I'll ever show up on the first ten pages of search results when someone Googles it.

It's also useful to consider the availability of domain names and social media accounts. Using a website like namechk.com you can type in the podcast name you want and instantly see whether that name is available as a domain, and as a handle on Twitter, Facebook, Instagram and about a hundred other platforms.

If you choose a name without going through this step, you may end up not being able to get a domain name for your website that people will associate with your podcast, and you may end up having to have different social media handles for each of the different platforms, which makes it difficult for people to find you.

Finally, you're going to be saying the name a lot, so choosing one that's easy to say and preferably easy to spell will save a lot of hassle in the future.

Choosing a podcast media host

Contrary to (somewhat) popular belief, you don't upload your podcast directly to Apple Podcasts, Spotify, or whichever app you usually use to listen to them. All those apps are simply ways to access audio that's hosted by media hosting companies.

While it is technically possible to self-host a podcast on your own servers, I wouldn't recommend it because there are so many excellent podcast media hosts that will do a great deal of the work for you and make the process ridiculously easy by comparison. There are options available for every budget, and the one you pick really is a personal decision to you.

At the end of the chapter is a table of some of the most popular media hosting sites, that will hopefully show you what you get for your money with the different options. When you're deciding on which host to go with make sure that you have a look at some of the shows that already host with that platform. Have a look at what kind of basic website they get from the host if you're planning on using that (although you should definitely plan to have your own site. More about why later) and also listen to the quality of the audio from several of the shows on the host to make sure that they are acceptable.

One thing that you'll notice is that some hosts limit the amount you can upload per month (presumably in the hope you'll upgrade to a more expensive tier) so you might be wondering how MBs translate into minutes. The truth is, it depends on a number of factors — what bitrate you use when you export your audio; whether your podcast is mono or stereo; even which software you use to edit.

As a rule of thumb, an hour of audio will probably result in an mp3 file between forty and sixty MBs, but be careful – your mileage may vary.

	Price per month	Integrates with Chartable	Website	Multiple Shows on same login	Monthly upload limit	IAB certified analytics	Site helps with monetization	Multiple team members	Monthly download limit	Transcription	Dynamic Ad insertion
Acast 'Starter'	Free		Basic		∞	✓			∞		
Acast 'Influencer'	$15		Customisable		∞	✓	Ad marketplace (US podcasts only)		∞		
Anchor	Free		Basic		∞				∞		
Blubrry 'Small'	$12		Customisable		100MB	✓			∞		
Blubrry 'Medium'	$20		Customisable		250MB	✓			∞		
Buzzsprout	$12	✓	Customisable	✓	3 hours		Affiliate marketplace	✓	∞	$0.25 per minute	
Buzzsprout	$18	✓	Customisable	✓	6 hours		Affiliate marketplace	✓	∞	$0.25 per minute	
Castos	$16	✓	Customisable	✓	∞				∞	$0.10 per minute	
Libsyn	$15	✓	Basic		250MB		Ad marketplace (5K+ US monthly downloads)		∞		
Podbean	$9	✓	Customisable		∞		Ad marketplace		∞		
Redcircle	Free		Basic	✓	∞		Ad marketplace		∞		✓
Simplecast	$13.50	✓	Customisable	✓	∞	✓		2	10,000		
Transistor	$16	✓	Customisable	✓	∞			3	10,000		
Whooshkaa Free	Free		Basic		∞	✓	Ad marketplace (Top 10% of podcasts)		1,000	Free - 1 hour per month	✓
Whooshkaa Semi-Pro	$29		Basic	2	∞	✓	Ad marketplace (Top 10% of podcasts)		10,000	Free - 2 hours per month	✓

2. Equipment

Microphones and audio interfaces

There's a lot of microphones out there and a lot of advice on which microphone is best for podcasting. I'm not going to list all of the options, because honestly there are only a few that make sense for beginner podcasters who are looking for good quality audio.

The main two types of podcast microphone are known as 'condenser' and 'dynamic' microphones. They work in different ways and they're each designed for slightly different purposes. But they're both great for podcasting in the right circumstances.

Condenser microphones are designed to be quite sensitive and pick up good quality quiet sounds, whereas dynamic microphones are designed more for loud sounds like drums, but they can also work really well with strong vocals such as someone sitting close to the microphone.

The advantage of a dynamic microphone over a condenser is that in most people's home podcasting setup, there is likely to be some background noise and dynamic microphones, because they are designed to be less sensitive, will pick up less of that extraneous noise than a condenser microphone.

Condensers are great in studios, or areas that are well treated for sound absorption and when there is very little background noise. Even in a standard home setup you can still get good quality sound from a condenser microphone, but you might have to do a bit more post-processing to remove some of that room noise

By far the most popular condenser microphone that is used for podcasting is the Blue Yeti, which you can get for just over $100.

Some podcasters can be a bit snobby about the Yeti, but in most cases, they probably can't tell if one is being used. The quality that you get is really good, and if you're careful about minimising your background noise and treating your audio in post-production, then you can get a really good professional result from a Blue Yeti.

It's a very easy mic to use, and like many condenser microphones it uses a USB cable to plug directly into your laptop or computer.

With dynamic microphones, one of the most popular options for podcasters is the ATR2100 from Audio Technica, which is also around $100.

It's a great quality microphone, with a good sound, and one of the great benefits to this microphone is that it can be used with

USB or XLR, so you can plug it directly into your laptop or into a mixer or audio interface.

XLR is a professional audio cable, and in the future, if you choose to upgrade your podcasting setup you may end up wanting to use XLR, so having the option on the ATR2100 is a good bonus.

The ATR2100 can occasionally be difficult to get hold of outside of the U.S. So, a good alternative is the Samson Q2U which is also USB and XLR compatible, and a great quality microphone.

If you're doing a solo podcast, or if you're podcasting with a co-host over the internet or interviewing guests over the internet, then a USB microphone is the main piece of equipment you need.

However, if you are podcasting with a co-host or guests in the same room or studio, there are some other considerations.

While in some cases it is possible to plug two USB microphones into one PC or Mac and be able to record them both on separate tracks, it can be very difficult, and the organisation or arrangement within your recording software can be temperamental, confusing and error prone.

Although using two different brands of USB microphones can help with this there are some other options.

One, if you have the ability to do so, is to have each person speaking into a different microphone, which is plugged in to a different PC or Mac. Each person can then record only their own audio, and those tracks can be transferred and edited together in the final podcast.

One drawback of this situation is that each computer has its own timing device, and over a long recording session it can mean that those audio tracks go out of sync, so some adjustment may need to be made when editing, to keep them synced up.

To avoid that problem and be able to record both sets of audio on one computer, the best solution would be to go through an audio interface which, in most cases, will be a piece of hardware, like a mixer, that accepts multiple inputs from different microphones and sends a signal out to your computer.

Often, these audio interfaces will accept XLR inputs rather than USB inputs, so the decision to use an audio interface will probably have an impact on your choice of microphone as well.

There are many types of audio interface designed for recording music, and some that are more specifically designed for podcasting.

In researching this you might be tempted by the recently released Rodecaster Pro. It certainly looks cool, and has some features that will definitely simplify your workflow, such as recording multi-track audio directly to an SD card. However, for most beginners the $500+ price tag probably outweighs the benefits of this device.

One of the most popular audio interfaces is the Focusrite Scarlett 2i2, which is available for around $140. It has two XLR mic inputs with separate gain controls and connects to your computer via USB for easy audio recording.

However, if your budget doesn't stretch that far there's also a large number of second-hand devices on the market which will do a similarly good job.

A final alternative option, which is probably more expensive than most people really need, is to use a hardware digital audio

recorder such as a Zoom H5 or Tascam DR-40. These have XLR inputs for two microphones and record directly to an SD card, so you don't even need recording software on your computer.

However, many digital audio recorders can also be used as audio interfaces, and if you *can* record on your computer as well as on the SD card then you have a backup and are less likely to run into audio problems down the road.

If you need more than two mic inputs the Zoom H6 has four – but the upgrade will cost you around $100 extra.

Headphones

Once you have your microphone sorted, the next item on your shopping list should be a good quality set of headphones.

Even if you're a solo podcaster, it's important to be able to hear your own voice while you're recording so that you can tell the quality and the volume that is coming through the microphone. If you are podcasting with a co-host remotely, over the internet, then a set of headphones is absolutely essential to avoid the feedback loop of your co-host's audio coming out of your speakers and back into your microphone. The same goes for remote guest interviews.

When choosing headphones for podcasting, make sure that they are closed back headphones that go over your ears, so that they minimise the amount of sound leakage. A long cord is useful, so that you're not too restricted in your movements. Ideally, you should also wear headphones when editing as the majority of people who listen to your podcast will probably be listening through headphones.

Mic stands and boom arms

Unless you're going to hold your microphone the whole time (bad idea, by the way – 'hand noise' can be transferred through the body of the mic), you'll need a microphone stand of some kind.

One of the advantages of the Blue Yeti is that it has a microphone stand built in, but for most other microphones you'll have to buy one.

You can buy a stand that sits on top of your desk or table or one that stands on the floor. A floor stand can be useful if you tend to fidget or if you'll be making notes or typing while you record, as some desk stands can transmit the noise from the desk surface into the microphone. Whether using a desk stand or a floor stand, make sure the microphone is in a comfortable position before you start recording as trying to move it during the record will be unacceptably noisy.

Another alternative is a suspension boom arm, which is increasingly popular among podcasters. A boom arm is typically hinged in the middle and tension is maintained with springs, allowing you to position your microphone pretty much anywhere you like, and while  there may still be a little movement noise it is easier to reposition even during a recording.

It attaches to the edge of your desk, or even better, to a nearby surface separate from your desk to avoid sound transmission. It frees up desk space when compared to a desk stand, and it's a lot more compact and easily stored and transported than a floor stand. It also removes the possibility of accidentally kicking or knocking the stand.

You don't have to spend a lot of money on a boom arm. But you should make sure that it is able to take the weight of your microphone. You can use a boom arm for a Blue Yeti but be aware the Yeti is a bulky and quite heavy mic, so you might want to find one specifically designed for it.

Pop filters

You'll need some kind of pop filter to get rid of the plosive sounds that you will make when saying words that start with B, P, T and similar letters.

You'll get some benefit from the foam windshield type cover that goes over the head of your microphone, but it's even better to use the kind that looks like a piece of fabric stretched across a frame, which often can be attached to your microphone stand or boom arm via some kind of gooseneck flexible arm.

You can spend a large amount on pop filters – I've seen them on sale for more than $50 – but it's totally unnecessary. All you need is a shield between your mouth and the capsule of the microphone, and a $10 pop filter will do the exact same job as a much more expensive one.

Ideally, this kind of pop filter should be placed so that it's around two to four inches from the microphone in order to allow room for the air to disperse after it goes through the fabric.

Sound treatment

You might want to think about some kind of sound treatment for the area where you'll be podcasting, and which kind you use will depend partly on whether you're setting up a permanent area for recording or whether you're just taking over a corner of your house for a couple of hours.

What we're talking about here is not sound proofing. Stopping the sound from coming through walls or windows takes a great deal more work, money, and potentially a construction job. Sound treatment is about removing echoes and reflections to maximise the quality of your audio.

Sit in the chair where you're planning to record, and look around. Imagine any flat surfaces you can see are mirrors. If you would be able to see yourself in those mirrors, then the sound coming out of your mouth when you talk will bounce off those surfaces and potentially into your microphone, muddying up the quality of your podcast. This is especially true if you're using a condenser mic, which will pick up more of the background noise.

If there are a lot of flat surfaces around you – especially shiny ones like windows – it might be time to have a look for somewhere else to record.

However, there are other things you can do. If you have curtains, draw them across the windows. Furniture in the room will absorb some sound, whether that's soft furnishings like a couch, or even bookcases full of books. You can hang blankets on walls or drape them over tables. And a carpeted room will usually be better than one with hard floors.

You can get dense blankets which are specifically designed to absorb sound – Producers Choice blankets are a good brand, from websites such as vocalboothtogo.

If you're going to set up a permanent area for podcasting you could attach fabric acoustic panels to your walls, or even use acoustic foam tiles like the ones you see on the walls of radio studios.

When we started recording *Fallacious Trump*, the only room I could record in without disturbing my family was a conservatory – which is just about the worst possible recording space. I made a DIY vocal booth by covering the inside surfaces of a large cardboard box with acoustic foam and sticking my microphone inside. It avoided some reflection and was better than no treatment at all, but I'm happy to say I've moved on from that now!

Field recording

An extra bit of kit that could come in handy if you're planning on doing interviews outside of your home or studio - perhaps at a conference or an event — is the Rode SC6-L Mobile Interview Kit.

The kit contains a couple of great quality Rode lavalier (tie-clip) mics and an adapter to plug them both into your iPhone or iPad.

You can get the whole kit for under $200, and when you use the free Rode Reporter app, you can record an interview very easily and at surprisingly high quality, even with quite a lot of background noise. With the adapter, you can even plug a pair of headphones in as well, so that you can monitor the audio, and the app even lets you record each microphone on a different audio track for easier editing later.

One of my clients has recorded several interviews this way in cafes and other public areas and has had great results.

3. Pre-production

Should I just make it up as I go along?

One thing that varies dramatically between different people, is to what extent they choose to plan their podcast episodes.

Authors sometimes talk about being either 'plotters' or 'pantsers'. Plotters lay out everything that's going to happen in their plot in a detailed outline before they start writing the book, while pantsers write by the seat of their pants (hence the name). They know generally the direction it's going; they may even have a destination in mind, but mostly they start writing and see where it takes them.

Similarly, with podcasting, some people will literally script every single word they're going to say in the episode, and others will essentially wing it the entire time. And there's a huge amount of grey area in between.

Ultimately, you need to decide what's right for you, and the chances are you'll fall somewhere between the two extremes.

If you're talking about something scientific or historical with a lot of details, you may choose to script everything to make sure you don't make mistakes, or you may be able to get by with just some detailed notes – especially if you know your subject well.

If you're making a comedy podcast, and your more skilful at writing jokes than improvising, a script is probably the way to go.

One note of caution: unless you're a trained performer, it can be difficult to read a script and make it sound like you're not reading a script. I would say that in most cases people don't want to listen to a script being read, so if that is how you come across when you're reading, then you might want to think about trying to plan it more in terms of bullet points or shorter sections that you plan out in advance, with some ad-libbing around those areas.

On the other extreme, if your show involves a few friends getting together to talk about what beer they like, or the latest sportsball game then you might be tempted to avoid any advance planning at all. Especially if you have strong opinions or a great deal of knowledge on a topic, then it might be easy for you to talk extemporaneously.

Even in this situation, however, I would recommend at least sticking to a consistent format for each episode. If nothing else, it's likely to make the editing easier than if you end up with an open-ended conversation that meanders from topic to topic with no conclusions or structure.

For *Fallacious Trump* we use a combination of bullet points (which remind us about stuff we've researched before recording), prepared audio clips which we then discuss, and some scripted sections.

If you're interviewing a guest, it's a good idea to script a brief introduction in which you talk about your guest's experience or achievements – basically to explain why they're on your show – and have some questions written down in advance. But don't rigidly stick to your questions if the conversation goes in an interesting direction – engage with your guest and explore what they have to say.

If you do choose not to script your podcast, then don't mistake a lack of a script for lack of research. Unless you're talking about a topic that is just your opinion or a subject you know really well. It's likely you're going to have to do some research, whether it's finding out about a guest, watching the TV episode you're talking about, or reading some news articles about a topic that you're going to cover that's relevant to current events.

Having done that research in advance, you can then choose how much detail you need to have in front of you when you actually sit down to record your podcast.

Intros

We've been conditioned over years of TV shows – particularly reality, news or documentary style shows, to expect an introduction to let us know what we're watching and what to expect. Rarely does a show begin without any acknowledgment of which show you're watching, who the hosts are or at least some theme music.

You may choose to have a brief standard opening for all your episodes, whether that's theme music or a voiceover, and then introduce the episode itself to give people an idea of what they're going to get out of listening to you.

When choosing how much information to put in your intro, keep it short. Make sure that it doesn't take too long to get to the thing that people have come to listen to.

If you spend ten or fifteen minutes talking about your day, or what you've been reading or drinking or whatever, that week, then people are going to either fast forward to the bit that they've come to listen to or turn off and not come back. Some podcasts do admittedly get away with this, but they tend to be shows which have earned a very loyal audience over several years, many of whom listen because they like the hosts themselves.

One thing that some podcasters do for their standard opening (as opposed to the episode specific portion) is have another person - such as a professional voiceover artist - do the introduction voiceover.

For example, Mark Dawson's podcast *The Self Publishing Show* starts with a bit of music under a short (fifteen seconds or so) clip from the author interview you're about to hear. Then the voiceover kicks in, still with a music bed:

> *Publishing is changing. No more gatekeepers. No more barriers. No-one standing between you and your readers. Do you want to make a living from your writing? Join indie bestseller Mark Dawson and first-time author James Blatch as they shine a light on the secrets of self-publishing success. This is The Self-Publishing Show. There's never been a better time to be a writer.*

And that's it. Forty seconds in everyone, including new listeners, knows exactly what podcast they're listening too, why they should keep listening and who the hosts are, and they've even heard a quick preview of this episode.

Having a professional VO artist can make your podcast sound much more professional very quickly, but some podcasters may prefer the personal touch of recording their own intro. Each approach is equally valid, and just depends on the kind of show you have and your relationship with your audience.

You might be thinking a professional voiceover artist would be expensive, but you'd probably be surprised. Voice123 is a fantastic marketplace where you can post a script for free and request auditions. You can either tell them your budget upfront or get voiceover artists to quote for the job. For a short script like the one above you'll get plenty of auditions even offering around $50.

You could, of course, take your chances on Fiverr – there are certainly many VO artists offering their services there, but make sure you listen to their samples and be prepared to pay for any changes or retakes.

You can even get a custom podcast intro, with voiceover, music and sound effects, produced by companies such as Music Radio Creative.

Music and stings

If you use music for your intro theme or for short 'stings' between segments, you're going to want to make sure that it's royalty free.

Royalty free music has been produced specifically for other creatives such as podcasters and video producers to use in their projects. While it is still copyrighted (as is any creative work you produce), when you buy or download the music you are also getting a licence to use it without paying additional royalties every time it is used.

If you want to use a piece of music that has not specifically been offered royalty free or under some kind of Creative Commons licence, you're not going to be able to do that without getting permission and probably paying a great deal of money, or potentially infringing copyright which could get you into trouble.

If you're making a podcast about a TV show, you can't use the show's theme tune. Even if a Beatles track, a Rihanna track, or a record released by a one-hit-wonder in the 80s that nobody's ever heard of is absolutely ideal for your podcast, tough. You can't use it without permission.

The good news is that there is a lot of really good quality royalty free music available for just a few dollars a track from sites like AudioJungle or there's even free music at Free Music Archive.

Be sure to check the licence of any tracks on FMA that you might want to use, as some do not allow use on podcasts, but most do.

Finally, try to make sure that when you choose some music, it fits with the tone of your podcast. So, if you're quite a casual fun podcast, you might not want to choose classical music, but if you are a professional business podcast, you probably don't want to pick some country music, or reggae.

Playing music or audio clips

Sometimes you might want to play some audio clips on your podcast. If it's just theme music or a sting to separate different sections, you can add them during the edit. But if, for example, you wanted to play a clip from a news story for you to discuss with your guest or co-host, then you'll need to do it in a way that means they can hear it too.

That's no problem if you're in the same room, but if you're recording remotely and you want to play multiple clips, you'll need some kind of soundboard. This is a piece of software or, in some rarer cases a piece of hardware, where you have audio clips associated with particular buttons or hot keys on your keyboard. When you want to play the audio you just press the button and it plays.

As you'll see from the table of remote recording options in Chapter 4, a couple of them have soundboards built in, so that you can upload pieces of audio that you want to play, and they will be audible to your guests and recorded alongside your microphone audio without needing any additional software. However, unless you use those specific programs, in most cases your co-host or guest will only hear the audio from your microphone, and not any audio you play on your computer during the call.

If you're using a mixer or audio interface, one handy option is an app for tablets, called I-Jingle. It's available on both Android and iOS tablets, and it's free (although there is a paid version, which has a bit more functionality).

You can run an audio cable directly out of the headphone jack on your tablet and into your mixer and play up to 30 different audio clips using the app.

If you're recording using a USB microphone, with no mixer, then you'll need some kind of soundboard software on your PC or Mac instead. But you'll also need an additional piece of software so that your remote recording site or your digital audio workstation can record the audio you're playing as well as your microphone.

There are lots of options, but I think one of the best for PC users is a free soundboard program called Resanance, which uses customisable hotkeys to play whatever audio you choose.

To get that audio to your recorder, a virtual mixer called Voicemeeter from VB audio, will allow you to take multiple inputs, such as your mic and your PC audio, and route them through to an aggregated virtual input that you can record.

For Macs, the best solution is a range of software from a company called Rogue Amoeba, which includes a soundboard called Farrago, and a virtual audio router called Loopback. Unfortunately, unlike the PC options, these aren't free – the two together will set you back around $150 plus local taxes, but they represent a really good quality solution for being able to play clips that your guests or co-host will hear, while also recording the audio.

Outro

As with the intro, you may also want to get a voiceover artist to do your outro and call to action, or you might want to do that yourself and make it different in every episode.

The main things that you want to remember when writing your outro are to let people know where else they can find more about you or your guest, or how to get in touch with you. If you write show notes with links to things you've talked about during the podcast, then this is a great time to let your listeners know where to find the show notes.

You might want to have a consistent sign-off line that you say at the end of the episode, or you might just want to thank people for listening.

When choosing your call to action for the outro, it's a good idea to ask your listeners to do just one thing per episode. Rather than saying they should subscribe and leave you a review and support you on Patreon and contact you on Twitter and all of the other things that you would like them to do, if you just choose one of the things each episode, then it's actually more likely that more of your listeners will do it.

How to interview people.

Interview podcasts are extremely popular, and it may at first seem like it's quite easy to just have a chat with someone, but actually interviewing is a skill.

You can get better at it with practice, but there are some things that you can think about beforehand that will make it easier.

One of the great things about doing an interview podcast is that in almost all circumstances you will know who you're going to be interviewing in advance. That means you have the opportunity to do a bit of research into them. You can read the information on their own website or their social media pages or listen to other interviews they've done. If they have a book that they are promoting. You should try to read the book if you can, or at least skim the book to get an idea of what is involved what the main ideas of the book are. If you like, you can ask them in advance about what topics they would like to cover.

Confirm the time and date of the interview in advance and give them a link to the page where you're going to be recording if that's how you work or your Skype address if you're going to be recording over Skype.

Before you start, have a think about what kinds of questions you're going to ask and write down some original questions that they don't get asked in every interview. If it's clear that they are there to talk about a particular topic, whether it's a book that they are promoting, or their area of expertise, make sure you're asking them questions that allow them to talk about that topic.

Ask open questions - ones that can't be answered with "yes" or "no" or another single word answer. Some sources that you read will tell you open questions start with who, what, why, where or how, but it's not quite that simple. In many cases questions that start with who or where can certainly be answered very briefly.

Think about questions which will prompt a longer answer, an anecdote or something useful to your audience. Let's imagine you have a podcast about sailing and you're interviewing someone who just sailed round the world single handed.

Some bad questions would be:

- How long did it take you?
- Did you get lonely?
- What kind of boat did you use?

Some good questions would be:

- Tell me about your lowest point on the journey.
- How did you cope with the solitude?
- Explain how you felt when you realised you were going to make it.

Talk to them briefly, if possible, before you actually start recording to give them a chance to relax and get used to talking to you a little bit before jumping straight in at the deep end.

Make sure that you're enthusiastic - keep your energy levels high and they will match your energy.

Let your guests talk. This interview is not about you, and it's not about showing how much you know, or how clever, or funny you are. You've chosen to have this guest on your podcast for a reason, so let them drive the conversation, while you guide where it goes with your questions.

Make sure that at the end of the interview you give them an opportunity to tell people where they should go to find out more about them – like their website - or to plug their book or podcast or whatever they have to promote.

And finally – here's the most important thing you can do when interviewing someone. If you forget everything else in this chapter, remember this: **Listen**.

Listen to your guest, and if you find something interesting, ask them a follow up question. Feel free to go down a rabbit hole that you weren't expecting. If it turns out to go nowhere you can always edit it out later, but sometimes you'll strike gold. Really listening will make your guest feel more comfortable and make them enjoy the conversation more, and that will come across in the audio.

The worst interviewers will work their way down a list of questions, just waiting for the guest to finish talking so that they can ask the next question, and sometimes they'll even miss the fact that their next question has already been answered. That kind of interview leaves the guest wondering why they bothered answering.

How to find guests

You might be surprised to know that the main thing you have to do to get guests to come on your podcast is just to ask them. In many cases, people will be happy to be asked and happy to be involved.

So, step one is to make list of people in your niche who you would like to interview, and go ahead and ask.

When you contact these people, write a brief and specific pitch email, telling them why you think that your audience would be interested in hearing what they have to say. Ideally if you have some way of giving them a reason to come on your show, such as the opportunity to promote their latest book or their own podcast or whatever, that would also be really useful to include.

Make sure that you include some detail specifically about them, such as an article of theirs you enjoyed, or another interview you heard them give. By making it specifically relevant to them, you're showing them it is a personal email and then it doesn't just look like you've sent the same email to fifty different people and hoped for the best.

You can also include in the email a link to an online booking software such as Calendly, where you can give people the opportunity to choose a time slot for an interview. The more flexible you can be about timeslots, the more successful you'll be in getting guests, at least until you're so big and famous that people are asking you if they can come on your show.

Once you've exhausted your wish-list of people that you would like to interview, here are some more places to look for suitable people.

- **Other podcasts in your niche.** The hosts of those podcasts are likely to be interested in appearing on your show, as it will help spread the word about their podcast as well. Also, if you hear any interesting guests on their shows, you should contact the guest, let them know that you heard their interview, and ask if they would be interested in appearing on your podcast. It's likely to be a yes, since they've already shown they're happy to be on a podcast!
- **Amazon.** Look up books that are relevant to your podcast topic, or that you believe your audience would like to hear about. Authors are always looking for more ways to get exposure for their books, and especially if they've been published quite recently, they will be glad of the opportunity to be interviewed, so they can position themselves as experts in their field.
- **Magazines.** If there are magazines that cover the same subject as your podcast, congratulations! This is an ongoing source for great guests. You can contact either the people who are writing articles in the magazines or the people they interview, because those are clearly people with some area of expertise in your subject.
- **Live events.** You may find there are conferences or events connected to your topic. For example, if you teach people about social media marketing, there are national and international events where people go to learn about social media marketing, and you can look at their websites and find out who is giving talks at those events. Even if you can't attend the event in person, you can still contact them, mention the event and the subject of their talk, and invite them on your podcast to talk more about it.
- **Facebook groups.** Aside from groups that are relevant to your niche, there are several Facebook groups specifically aimed at connecting podcast hosts with potential interview guests. The three biggest and most

useful ones are called *Podcast Guest Experts*, *Podcast Guest Connection*, and *I'll Guest For That Podcast*.

- **Guest booking sites and services**. There are lots of sites which are set up specifically to cater to people looking to be interviewed by the press, on radio shows, or on podcasts, and almost all of them also help hosts find guests, with either a directory of their clients or sometimes even an email list you can sign up to. Most of these sites are free for hosts, because they make their money charging potential guests, who are often happy to pay for the exposure they will gain. The following list covers the main sites and gives an idea of costs on both sides, because you'll want to refer back here when we talk about marketing your podcast!

    o Matchmaker.fm – Hosts free; Guests free
    o SpotaGuest.com – Hosts free; Guests free
    o Poddit.net – Hosts free; Guests freemium
    o AwesomeGuests.com – Hosts free; Guests freemium
    o InterviewGuestDirectory.com – Hosts free; Guests from $5.95 per month
    o PodcastGuests.com – Hosts free; Guests from $99 per year
    o RadioGuestList.com – Hosts free; Guests $29 per month + $229 one-off fee
    o ExpertBookers.com – Only for guests – from $500 per month!
    o InterviewValet.com/host – Hosts free; Guests from $750 per month!!!!
    o Kitcaster.com – Only for guests – from $1000 per month!!!!!!!!

4. Production

DAWs (Digital Audio Workstations)

When you actually come to produce your show, one of the first things you'll need is some recording software. This is often referred to as a digital audio workstation, or DAW. But basically, it's just audio recording and editing software.

In the table that follows this section, I've laid out some of the most common pieces of software that are used for recording podcasts. I've restricted it to programs that can be used to both record and edit, because while there are some solutions which only do one of those things, I don't think there's much sense in having to learn two different programs - one to record and one to edit your podcast. You might as well just learn one program, get really good at it and be able to do all of the things you need to do.

Which program is right for you, is very much a matter of personal preference. The ones that aren't free all have free trials, so if you want to try them out, you can. Whichever you pick, all of these programs contain all you need to record and edit a podcast. I'm not going to go into detail on how to use them all, because you can find great tutorials online for pretty much anything you need to do, created by people with far more specialist knowledge than me on the programs.

GarageBand is free, but limited, and some features such as multitrack recordings can be a bit hard to find.

Logic Pro X is the natural upgrade for Garage Band users (both are Mac only). Even though there are several more advanced features such as levelling and EQ, an easy to use noise reduction feature is still lacking.

By far the most popular free DAW is Audacity®. If you've never used an audio editing program before, the learning curve on  Audacity is fairly standard, but if you've used other programs you may find Audacity less intuitive, as it often doesn't do things in the same way as other programs. Similarly, if you end up moving away from Audacity in the future, you might find the skills you've acquired aren't that transferable. That said, many people swear by Audacity and it is used to edit some very popular and professional podcasts.

One thing to bear in mind is that, unlike all the other DAWs on this list, Audacity uses 'destructive editing', which means that any effects you apply, or cuts you make to the audio change the original file. You can undo a change, but if you trim a section out, then reduce the background noise, then level the audio, then apply some EQ, you can't adjust the trim without undoing everything else as well. With non-destructive editing, each of those changes can usually be undone or altered without having any impact on the others.

Hindenburg is designed for storytellers - for podcasters, radio journalists and audio book creators. In fact, the most basic version of Hindenburg is called Hindenburg Journalist. At $95, it's far from the most expensive option, but if you want some of the slightly more advanced options such as multitrack recording or noise reduction 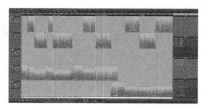 then you have to pay out a *lot* more to get Hindenburg Pro.

If you do make the investment, Hindenburg Pro's noise reduction is excellent - it continuously analyses your track and there's literally a single dial that you just need to turn to increase or decrease the amount of noise reduction.

Reaper is absolutely packed with different features, and for a relatively low price you get a very powerful DAW. This means that it can take a bit longer to learn than other programs, but once you master it there are very few limits to what you can do.

Finally, Adobe® Audition®, which is part of the Adobe Creative Suite. Due to the fact that Adobe only offers a subscription option, this ends up being one of the more costly choices, at $20 per month, every month. You don't own Audition; you just pay a license to continue to use it. The price puts a lot of people off unless you happen to use other Adobe programs (I'm a video producer by day, so I use Premiere® and After Effects®), in which case Audition often comes as part of the bundle.

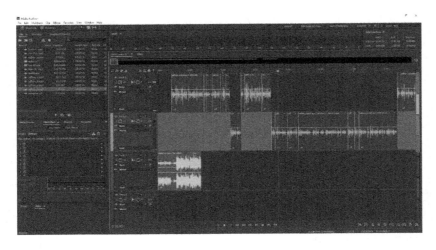

If you do have access to it, or aren't dissuaded by the price, you'll find Audition is an extremely powerful and versatile DAW that is

somehow also and easy to learn. This is helped somewhat by the fact there are probably more online tutorials available for Audition than any other DAW, but it's also helped by the intuitive design of the program.

	Price	PC	Mac	Multitrack recording	Noise reduction	Free trial
Garage Band	Free		✓			N/A
Logic Pro X	$200		✓	✓		90 days
Audacity	Free	✓	✓	✓	✓	N/A
Hindenburg Journalist	$95	✓	✓			30 days
Hindenburg Pro	$375	✓	✓	✓	✓	30 days
Reaper	$60	✓	✓	✓	✓	60 days
Adobe Audition	$20 per month	✓	✓	✓	✓	7 days

Remote recording

If you're planning to do a podcast where you have to talk to someone over the internet, whether that is your co-host or a guest that you're interviewing, or in some cases, both (you might have a co-hosted podcast where you also interview people), you're going to need some remote recording software.

If it's just you and a co-host you could plausibly just use some audio-conferencing software like Skype, and each of you can record locally on their own computers (into a DAW) or into a hardware recording device, such as a Zoom H5. Recording both ends of the conversation locally is called a 'double-ender' and will result in the best quality of overall audio.

However, you can't expect your interview guests to be able to record their end of the call. Fortunately, there are several software options that you can use that contain a VoIP system just like Skype, but which also allow you to record both ends of the call.

My co-host on *Fallacious Trump* lives in a different county to me, so we record over the internet. We both record our ends of the call locally (me using Audition, him using a hardware recorder), so we could theoretically speak over Skype, but instead we choose to use Zencastr. Apart from giving us the chance to talk to the occasional guests we have on the show, recording our conversation through Zencastr gives us some redundancy in case one of our local systems has a problem.

On the odd occasion that my software crashed, or the batteries on Mark's Marantz digital audio recorder ran out, it was a huge relief to have the Zencastr recordings so that our hilarious and highly intellectual dialogue wasn't lost forever.

The most common remote recording solutions that people use are laid out in the table at the end of this section.

Ecamm for Skype and Zoom.us handle the recording a bit differently from the others on the list. Essentially, they record everything going out of and into your computer during the call. That means that while your own audio quality will be great, you're recording your guest's audio after it's been compressed and sent over the internet to your computer, which might mean the quality suffers. If you've ever had connection problems during a Skype call or an online meeting, you can imagine how these would affect the recording you can make.

The other solutions on my list use a kind of virtual double-ender recording, where the audio is recorded locally at both ends. It's then uploaded to the website either during or after the call, and is available for you to download. This avoids connection problems because if the connection is lost, each person's recording is preserved on their computer until the connection is made again.

	Price	mp3	wav	Built in VOIP	Virtual double ender	Sound board	Video	Max no. of people on call	Time limit	Mac only	Online	Free trial
Cleanfeed	Free		✓	✓	✓			∞	∞		✓	N/A
Cleanfeed Pro	$22 per month		✓	✓	✓			∞	∞		✓	N/A
Clearcast	$25 per month	✓		✓	✓	✓		2	10 hrs per month		✓	20 minutes
Ecamm for Skype	$40	✓	✓				✓	4	∞	✓		7 days
Squadcast 'Dabbler'	$9 per month	✓	✓	✓	✓		Yes, but recording is audio only	4	2 hrs per month		✓	7 days
Squadcast 'Creator'	$17 per month	✓	✓	✓	✓		Yes, but recording is audio only	4	5 hrs per month		✓	7 days
Zencastr	Free	✓		✓	✓			3	8 hrs per month		✓	N/A
Zencastr Pro	$20 per month	✓	✓	✓	✓	✓		∞	∞		✓	N/A
Zoom	Free	✓		✓			✓	No limit on 2-person meetings, 40 min. per meeting limit on up to 100 people			✓	N/A

Minimizing ambient noise

Back in Chapter 2, when we talked about equipment, we talked about some of the ways in which you can maximize the quality of the audio that you're recording with sound treatment.

But it's also important when you're actually recording to think about the ambient noise in the room, or any external noises that might be interfering with your recording. With a little effort and forethought, it's easy to minimize this, and reducing the noise before you press record is *way* easier than fixing it in post.

For example:

- Consider the room. Remember that carpet, curtains and soft furnishings will give you a better sound than counters, windows and hard floors.
- Make sure that your children or pets are kept out of the area where you're recording
- Listen carefully before you start recording for any extraneous noises like loudly ticking clocks which can be taken down or moved.
- Don't run any appliances while you're recording such as dishwashers or washing machines.
- Close windows to reduce noise from traffic, airplanes or local wildlife.
- If you must record in the same room as a refrigerator, consider unplugging it for the duration of your recording.
- Turn off any air conditioning, ceiling fans, or heaters.
- If you have a computer with loud fans, place it as far away from the microphone as possible, and close all non-essential programs to prevent the fans from activating.

- To avoid getting an electrical buzz on your recordings, make sure all your recording equipment is plugged into the same power strip (with a surge protector) and keep your microphone cables well away from any electrical cables.
- Turn your phone off!

Mic technique

Another thing that has a significant effect on the quality of the audio that you'll be able to record is your microphone technique. Most people don't use microphones on a regular basis so may not have had any reason to think about this before.

Make sure that you're not touching your microphone at any point because with most microphones sound will travel through the casing and be audible on your track. Aside from having a mic stand or boom arm to hold your mic still, it's also really important to get your microphone placement right so that you don't have to touch it or move it while you're recording

The capsule of the microphone should be somewhere around three to five inches from your mouth, although mics have different sensitivity levels, so be prepared to experiment with this. Ideally, to avoid plosives and loud breathing noises, the microphone should be slightly off-axis.

Okay, what do I mean by 'off-axis'? If the microphone is in front of your face, pointing directly at your mouth and you talk directly into it, then all of your breath is also going directly into the diaphragm of the microphone. That's where you'll get some unpleasant breath sounds even with a pop filter.

When I say the microphone should be off-axis, I don't mean turning the microphone so that it isn't facing your mouth. The microphone should always be pointing directly at your mouth when you're talking. However, you can position it in a way so that your face is angled slightly away from the microphone, so that you're not talking directly into it - you're talking past it.

That way your breath is also going past it and not directly into the microphone. So long as the microphone is still pointed at your mouth, it will still pick up really good quality sound, but it won't have that unpleasant breath sound and plosive problems.

on-axis　　　　**off-axis**

Finally, move back slightly from the microphone when you're not talking, so that your breathing isn't picked up while your co-host or guest is talking.

5. Post Production

Editing

The main aspect of post producing your podcast will be done in the digital audio workstation you chose back in Chapter 4.

If you've recorded into a hardware recorder then you'll need to import that audio, but in all other cases the audio will be right there in your DAW, ready to be edited.

The amount of editing you need to do will vary dramatically depending on what kind of podcast you're making, how polished you want it to sound, and how efficient you were when you recorded it. But unless you happen to be an amazing natural presenter, you probably will need to do at least *some* editing in order to make your audio sound better, whether it's removing places where you stumbled over your words or messed up, or just taking out filler words like, 'um', 'like', 'you know', and so on. Sometimes there'll be a point where you and your co-host went off on a tangent, that might not be interesting to your listeners, or one of you made a joke that didn't land.

Those are the kinds of things you want to tighten up and edit out before you upload your audio to your media host. Basically, you're asking people to invest time to listen to your podcast, so don't waste their time; respect them and make sure that the material you're putting out is as tightly edited, and high quality as it can be.

You may want to do some audio sweetening, whether that is removing background noise, using an EQ filter on your voice to make it sound nicer, or levelling or compressing the audio to make sure your listeners don't need to keep turning the volume up and down.

Bitrates and LUFS

When you're mastering your podcast and exporting it in your DAW, you'll need to choose your file format, what bitrate you export it at, and a few other things.

While some media hosts accept other file types such as AAC, you'll find that by *far* the most widely accepted format for podcasts is the good old mp3.

Choosing a bitrate is basically a balancing act between getting a good quality sound and a small file size so that they download quickly and don't take up too much storage space. Some media hosts restrict the amount of storage they will give you or the amount that you can upload per month, and that is affected by the bitrate of your file. The bitrate is simply a measure of how much data is processed in a given amount of time, and it's measured in kilobits per second or kbps.

Fairly standard among podcasts, in order to get a good quality sound with a reasonably small file is to export at 64 or 96 kbps if it is a mono file. If you want to export in stereo, then 128 kbps is better.

Mono is usually a good choice for most podcasts unless you have a specific reason for exporting in stereo. Some podcasts, including *Fallacious Trump*, choose to put the each host slightly off-centre in the stereo mix, so that one host is more on the left channel and one is more on the right channel, which can help people to differentiate between the hosts and hear better when there's a little bit of crosstalk.

However, I would caution against panning the hosts too far off-centre or even restricting one fully to the left channel and the other fully to the right. In some cases, as headphones get older and start to fail, especially if they spend a lot of time coiled up in pockets or bags, one side of the headphones will stop working first. If one of your hosts is only on the left channel and my left earbud stops working, I can't listen to your podcast until I get some new headphones.

In terms of volume, when you're getting ready to export you can check the audio meter in your DAW and see that most of your audio peaks are somewhere between -6dB and 0dB.

> A brief aside, just in case you're interested – you might think it's odd that the decibels are measured in negative numbers, especially when you've probably heard things like *"a regular conversation is about 60dB, and a motorbike engine is 95dB"*. And yes, it is kind of odd. Suffice it to say that there are several different dB scales, but they all measure sound relative to a (different) fixed loudness. Those environmental sounds are relative (on a logarithmic scale!) to the lower threshold of human hearing, which is 0dB and that system is called dBA.
>
> Meanwhile, digital audio is measured in dBFS, or 'decibels relative to Full Scale', where 0dB is the highest possible signal level in a WAV file (a WAV is an uncompressed audio file format). At or above 0dB, the audio 'clips', which means that the waves are flattened at the top and bottom and a lot of detail is lost. So that means -6dB is six decibels below the maximum. OK, back to the stuff you actually need to know.

However, decibels are simply a measurement of the volume at any given moment. There's another system which looks at loudness across a longer period, and it's better at standardising how loud a podcast actually seems. That system is measured in LUFS (sometimes also called LKFS for reasons too boring to go into here) and whichever DAW you're using you should be able to specify the LUFS measurement of your file.

Apple has long recommended -19 LUFS for mono podcasts and -16 LUFS for a stereo podcast, but Spotify, Alexa devices and some podcast apps such as Overcast normalise all their audio (including podcasts) to -14 LUFS, so realistically anywhere in that range will be fine.

If all of that sounds a bit too complicated or annoying to be bothered with, read on!

Auphonic

If you don't want to rely too much on your own skills as an audio engineer in normalising, levelling, compressing and sweetening your audio, there is a handy solution, which I happen to love.

Auphonic is a web based app which you can upload your audio files to, whether it's a single track or multiple speakers, and it will level all of the audio so that it's the same volume across the whole episode; it will normalise your loudness to the LUFS setting that you specify; it will reduce noise and hum within the files; and it even has auto ducking features which mean that if you have an a music track that you want to be lower while you're talking, and then louder when you're not talking, it can do that automatically.

The online version also has an ID3 tagger so that you can tag your podcast with good quality metadata.

And the best thing of all is that you can get two hours of audio processed per month, absolutely free, and there are various options for buying extra time if two hours a month isn't enough for you.

Finally, there are even Auphonic desktop apps, which you pay for once, and then download for either PC or Mac, which will give you as much time as you need, with no restriction. The desktop apps are limited to *either* single track or multitrack processing, so you have to choose which one you want, whether you're a solo podcaster, or you have a co-host or guests. The desktop apps lose some of the functionality of the web app, such as ID3 tags, but they are quicker to use because you don't have to upload the audio, wait for the processing to happen, and then download the result - you can do it all on your computer.

ID3 tags

ID3 tags are a way of embedding metadata into an mp3 file. You can think of them as SEO for podcasts, and they are important for helping people discover your podcast in Apple Podcasts or other podcatchers, but they are also what allows your podcast app to display all the information about your episode while your podcast is playing.

You *can* use iTunes as an ID3 tag editor, by importing your audio file into iTunes, right-clicking on the file and choosing 'Get Info', but the tag editor within iTunes has some significant shortcomings including a very limited allowable length for descriptions.

Happily, there is a significantly better free tool called Mp3tag, which lets you edit all of the details that you need to.

Mp3tag is technically only available on PCs but it will run on a Mac through a compatibility program called Wine, and there are full instructions on how to do this on the Mp3tag website.

One of the elements of the ID3 tags is the description of the episode, which you can put as much or as little detail into as you want. It can be a really useful place to put links and information about the guests on an episode, or websites or books that you mentioned during the show. If you add timings, to your list of things that happened in the show, then it means that people who may be listening to your podcast for a particular element of it, or want to find out a specific thing you've talked about will know where they can go to.

Not all podcast apps will display these details in the same way, so it can be difficult to predict how people will actually see them, and not all will have usable hyperlinks that people will be able to click on with their phone, and go straight to a website.

When you need to put more information, post images, embed videos, or have links that you know people will be able to use, the best place to put all this is in your show notes.

Show notes

Your show notes are usually a longer and more detailed version of the description that you put in your ID3 tags, and you would usually house the show notes on your website.

It gives you an opportunity to give your listeners much more information or to link to things that you've said or done. It's also fantastic for SEO, and to help people discover your website, and therefore your podcast,

The show notes don't have to be extremely detailed; it can be just a list of bullet points of the things that you've talked about. Timestamps again can be great, because they can point people to directly to the information that they're looking for.

On your website you should make sure that you start your show notes by embedding a media player for your episode. All media hosting companies will give you an embeddable player that you can use to put onto your website page for that episode, so that people can find that page thanks to the show notes, and then listen to the episode there and then

The more detailed you make your show notes, the better it is for SEO, but again, make sure it's sustainable. It's important to be consistent and have the same kind of style, same level of detail, and ideally a consistent format, and it does greatly increase the content on your website, but if you end up not doing it because you are trying to be too ambitious, and it would take you too much time or you fall behind and miss several episodes because it's too much work, then essentially that's a negative.

It would be better to do more simple show notes with just an intro, some bullet points and a call to action at the end and be able to do that consistently so that there is the same kind of information for every episode.

Always make sure that if you have a guest on your podcast, you link out to where people can find more information about that guest. For example, if they're a podcast host you can link to their podcast or maybe they have a book or a website that you can point people towards. That way they will get something out of having been on your show and, hopefully, other guests who investigate your show before deciding whether to agree to an interview will see that you're trying to be helpful to your guests and get them some exposure.

Finally, your show notes are a great place to link to your transcript, if you choose to create one.

Transcripts

Unlike your show notes, a transcript is a document that features every single thing you say, not just in note form, but literally all of the words that you said on your show.

It's fantastic for SEO, because anything that you talk about in an audio file isn't consistently indexed by Google. (although they are working on that) but when you put it in text on your website, then it can be indexed by Google and people can find your website and then discover your show.

Apart from SEO, people also use transcripts if they are hard of hearing or deaf (yes, dDeaf people do listen to podcasts!), or if English isn't their first language. They may listen to your podcast and read along in the transcript.

Some media hosts offer transcription as part of their service to you or as an extra thing that you can pay for. But in the absence of that there are a lot of services which are really good at providing quality transcripts, and certainly a lot more easily than you spending your time listening back to everything that is said in your show and trying to type it out.

In the table at the end of this section, I've included some of the more common services that people use to get their podcasts transcribed and while they are mostly very good quality, you will often have to go through and correct some mistakes - but that's a lot quicker than trying to transcribe the podcast yourself.

The quality of your audio is key to the results you'll get. If you speak clearly and there isn't much background noise, you'll probably be pleasantly surprised by how accurate they are, even though only one on the list uses actual people to do the transcription.

To give you an idea of the relative accuracy of the different sites, I uploaded a short audio clip of our standard episode outro. The outro has 133 words, and here is how many of those words each site got correct. While there is some variation, they all did better than 93% accuracy, which is pretty good, since all except the human-transcribed one were finished within a couple of minutes (the human one took about twenty minutes). Remember, this was a fairly unscientific test – your mileage may vary.

Happy Scribe – 124
Otter – 125
Podcast Transcribe – 124
Rev (human) - 130
Rev (auto) – 126
Sonix – 129
Temi – 125
YouTube – 127

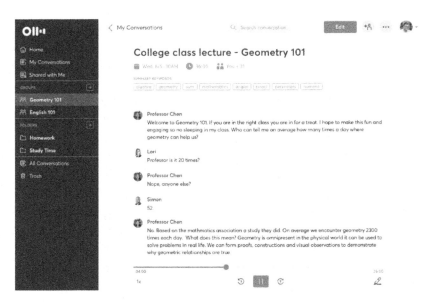

	Price	Add custom vocabulary	Identify speakers	Timestamps	Free Trial
Happy Scribe	€12 per hour		✓	✓	30 mins
Otter	Free for up to 120 minutes per month	✓	✓	✓	N/A
Otter Premium	$8.33 per month for 100 hours	✓	✓	✓	N/A
PodcastTranscribe.com	$5 per podcast		✓		-
Rev (human option)	$1.25 per minute	✓	✓	Extra 25¢ per min	-
Rev (automated)	$0.25 per minute				45 mins
Sonix	$10 per hour	✓	✓	✓	30 mins
Temi	25¢ per minute		✓	✓	45 mins
YouTube	Free				N/A

Audiograms

One thing that some podcast producers create as an extra way of getting their podcast out there, is a special kind of video called an audiogram. The audio is from your podcast – often a short highlight, but it can even be a whole episode, and the 'video' is often a static image, perhaps a logo of your show, with a moving waveform which dynamically represents the audio, and sometimes captions that follow along as well. If you've created a transcript then you can use that when creating the captions for your audiograms.

You can upload the resulting videos to YouTube, Facebook, Twitter or many other social media sites (although some have quite draconian restrictions on how long your videos can be). Clips can be used to promote your show, or uploading the full episode can give you another outlet where your podcast can be discovered.

There are three main companies that you can use to get these made, and it's worth looking at each to see which you think might be best for you.

In my opinion, by far the most useful is Headliner, which gives you ten free videos per month, and allows you to use your full episode if you wish, all the way up to two hours! It will also auto-transcribe your audio if you want.

Next is Wavve, which only gives you one minute of free video per month. Ten minutes is $10, and the price rises steeply from there.

The final company is Audiogram (who presumably got in early with the naming, and whose website can be found by searching for Get Audiogram), which gives you two free videos per month. They also will transcribe your video, but on their free service transcription is limited to videos lasting one minute, so if you want to use a clip that is sixty-one seconds or longer, you won't be able to have that transcribed.

Outsourcing

Post production is the area of podcasting which is most commonly outsourced. Sure, there are plenty of companies that will help you with various pre-production aspects of your podcast, such as consulting right from the very beginning to help you work out your podcast name, your cover art, your format, and your schedule, and that may be really, really useful if you think that you could benefit from having some help in that process.

However, for most people, if they choose to outsource some of their podcast production, it is going to be the editing and mastering, since that will free up the most time for them without relinquishing much control.

In many cases, you can just upload your audio files after you've recorded them, and the podcast
producer will edit, level, reduce noise, duck music, add your regular intro and outro and create the mp3 file.

Often, they will be able to add ID3 tags, and they might even write show notes for you if you like, as well as uploading your file to your media hosts, and maintaining your RSS feed (more about RSS feeds in a moment!) and distributing it.

If you have the budget, then this can be a way to podcast while saving a great deal of time, because this part of the process can be especially time consuming.

One huge benefit of podcast consulting/producing, is that it can be done completely remotely, so you don't have to have an office where your podcast consultant or producer can come to meet with you - you can do it all online. If you use a remote recording software such as the ones we talked about in the previous chapter, they can even listen in on your recording and be involved in that part of the process as well.

If you'd like to find out about my podcast consultation and podcast producing services, feel free to get in touch with me at jim@jimcliff.co.uk

6. Distribution

RSS feeds

Once you've uploaded your first episode to your media host, there's a bit more work to do before everyone can find it in their podcast apps. Some media hosts will let you 'automatically' submit your podcast to places like Apple, Spotify, Stitcher and others.

While this does seem easy, please avoid the temptation to go this route, because in many cases that removes an amount of control from you. That will become important later on if you choose to change media hosts, or make other changes to your podcast.

It's in fact extremely easy to take control of all of the distribution of your podcast, because your podcast host will give you an RSS feed URL (or web address) which is specific to your podcast.

An RSS feed is basically a script containing all of the information about your podcast - it contains all of the metadata for the show itself, the cover art, the location of all of the audio of your episodes, and all of the individual episode metadata.

Using that RSS feed, anyone who has an RSS reader can subscribe to your podcast, and podcast apps are basically just specialised RSS readers. Some apps draw their data directly from the Apple Podcasts directory while many have their own databases. That means that the more directories and apps you give your information to, the more discoverable your podcast will be.

Fortunately, you only need to tell each directory about your podcast once, and after that, every time you upload a new episode all the apps will be notified by your RSS feed, which your media host will automatically update.

Podcast Mirror

The first thing to do, before you start submitting your RSS feed to the various podcatchers, is to use a service called Podcast Mirror

Podcast Mirror is a free service, run by Blubrry, which is a very well-established podcast media host. They've been around since 2005, and are still very successful and likely to be around for a long time.

When you put your RSS feed URL into Podcast Mirror, they replicate your feed, and they will give you a new feed URL. This new URL is the one which you then submit to all of the podcast directories.

Why would you go through this extra step if all you're getting is another RSS feed?

Well, if for some reason, your circumstances change in years to come, and you decide you want to change your podcast media host, you don't have to go back and resubmit your RSS feed to all of the different sites that you've put it on. All you need to do is go into your Podcast Mirror account and put a new RSS feed in there. And your mirrored RSS address stays the same.

So, all of the podcast aggregators and directories who are looking for your RSS feed will still look in the same place, and they will be pointed directly through Podcast Mirror to your new feed.

It's like in the old days, when people had landlines (sadly, I'm old enough to remember this very well), when you moved to a new house you would often need to get a new phone line, and a new number. So, you'd have to tell everyone your new number – and since we used dial phones back then everyone needed to write down or remember your number. There was no speed dial!

Using Podcast Mirror is like moving to a new house, but keeping the same phone number, so everyone can still get in touch with you and knows where to find you.

Submitting to iTunes/Apple Podcasts

By far the most important place to submit your RSS feed to, once you have one from Podcast Mirror, is Apple Podcasts, and it's pretty simple to do.

You just go to podcastsconnect.apple.com and login with your iTunes account. If you don't have an iTunes account, then you can create one very easily.

You should submit to Apple first, because, apart from being the largest single place that people go to for podcasts, and the fact that many major podcast apps use the Apple directory, they're also the most strict in terms of getting your podcast accepted, so if you can get your podcast validated and accepted on Apple Podcasts then everywhere else will also accept it.

Once you're logged in on podcastsconnect, you click the 'plus' button to submit an RSS feed and paste your URL into the box.

It may take several days before your podcast is accepted, so if you are planning to launch your podcast on a specific day with a certain amount of fanfare, media coverage or promotional emails, you'll want to make sure you submit it to Apple in advance.

One thing you can do is upload a test episode – even a really short bit of audio. For example, you could just introduce the show and the hosts and let people know what the show will be about. Practically speaking, it very unlikely anyone will ever hear this test episode, because once your feed has been validated and accepted by Apple Podcasts, you can delete that test episode and upload your first real episode. Of course, if you want to, you can simply upload your first episode and wait for it to go through.

Apple will also need you to upload your cover art. None of the other directories really seem to mind much what is in your cover art, but the criteria from Apple are so strict that your cover art can cause your entire podcast feed to be rejected.

In the days after you submit your feed to Apple you can log back in to your podcastsconnect account to check the status. If you've been accepted then great, but if you've been rejected it will let you know whether it was your cover art or something else (although it won't always be very specific about exactly why!)

Cover art

When you're creating your cover art, here are the criteria that you need to fulfil in order to get accepted by Apple Podcasts.

- It needs to be square, and between 1400 x 1400 pixels and 3000 x 3000 pixels. In order to future proof your art, it's probably better to aim more towards the upper end of this range.
- JPEG or PNG files only.
- It needs to be 72 dpi.
- RGB colour space, not CMYK. And transparent PNGs don't work in Apple Podcasts.
- You are not allowed to use blurry or pixelated images.
- No explicit language, or references to drugs, profanity or violence in the image.
- No Apple products, words, or logos. (One of my clients had difficulty getting their feed accepted because they had used an iPad in their cover art. It took a while for us to figure out what we'd done wrong).

In terms of design, remember that when people are choosing whether or not to subscribe, or even listen to an episode of your podcast essentially all they'll see in most cases will be the name of the podcast and the cover art. So, try to make it as attractive and eye-catching as possible. Your cover art is the book cover that people will judge your book by.

It has to be representative of the subject that you are talking about, so if it's a business podcast, feel free to include your company logo. Take a look at other podcasts in your subject area. DO NOT copy their designs, but take note of which ones you find compelling, and why – which ones do you want to listen to?

Remember that, while the file you upload to Apple may be 3000 pixels square, almost nobody will ever see it that size. In fact, when people are browsing on the iTunes store or in other podcast apps, your art will probably be less than 100 pixels square. So, make sure the image is clear even at small sizes, and don't use too much text. Make sure the text you do use is in a font that is clearly legible, even at smaller sizes, and use contrasting colours to make it stand out from the background.

Try to avoid clichés like microphones and headphones, unless you're specifically making a podcast about podcasting or audio engineering or something like that, because there are so many podcasts that use those icons in their cover art, when it isn't relevant, and essentially it's like showing some paper on the cover of a book or a movie camera on a movie poster. It doesn't really make any sense.

You will see when you look at cover art for other podcasts, a lot of people use their faces. If the podcast, really is just about you talking and there aren't any other elements to it that you could illustrate visually in the cover art, then perhaps a picture of you would work.

If you're famous, or even if you already have a following in your niche and people would recognise your face, then by all means use your face on the cover art. But really, in the absence of that, I don't know that it makes a great deal of sense to have your face on the cover art if people don't know who you are. There's no particular reason why it would make anyone want to listen to your podcast.

Distribution to podcast apps & directories

Once you have your feed accepted by Apple, then you're ready to distribute it to other podcatchers, and podcast directories.

When you look online, you'll find various lists of places you can submit your feed to but unfortunately, many of them are incomplete or out of date. I believe the list below represents the most comprehensive list of directories and podcast aggregators who are currently accepting submissions in May 2020.

If you submit it to all of these places you will be doing very well, and your podcast will be as 'findable' as possible. If you don't want to take the time to go to all of these websites and give them your RSS feed, then at least go to the ones in bold. TuneIn is particularly important if you want to be available to people through smart speakers like Amazon's Alexa. If you ask Alexa to play a particular podcast, she'll check TuneIn for it first.

- acast.com/en/app
- addictpodcast.com/submit
- ampplaybook.com/podcasts
- anypod.net/publish
- beyondpod.com/forum (Join the forum and post your apple podcasts link)
- blubrry.com/addpodcast.php
- bullhorn.fm/podcasters
- castbox.fm/podcasters-tools
- digitalpodcast.com/feeds/new
- himalaya.com/claim
- hubhopper.com (Click 'Add/Remove' in the header)
- iheart.com/content/submit-your-podcast

Starting a Podcast in 2020

- ipodder.org/hints/new
- laughable.com/artist-resources (Email your feed URL to info@laughable.com)
- learnoutloud.com (Only for educational podcasts. Email your feed URL to podcast@learnoutloud.com)
- listenapp.co (Click on 'I'm a podcaster' in the header, you'll be sent an email with instructions)
- listennotes.com/submit
- luminarypodcasts.com (Email your name, your podcast's name, your feed URL and your iTunes URL to submissions@luminarypodcasts.com)
- partners.stitcher.com/join
- player.fm/add
- pocketcasts.com/submit
- podbean.com/site/submitPodcast
- podcast.app (Email your feed URL to help@podcastapp.io)
- podcasters.breaker.audio
- podcasters.deezer.com/submission
- podcasters.radiopublic.com
- podcasters.spotify.com/submit
- podcastex.com/addpodcastform.asp
- podcastgang.com (Click 'Suggest Podcast' in the footer)
- podcastrepublic.net/for-podcast-publisher
- podcastsmanager.google.com/add-feed
- podchaser.com/podcasts (Click 'Add Podcast' in the footer)
- podfanatic.com/podcast/create
- podknife.com (Sign up, then choose 'Suggest a podcast' from the menu)
- podmust.com (Click 'Submit a podcast' in the header)
- podtail.com (Choose 'Suggest a podcast' from the menu)
- shorturl.at/cnWX6
- spreaker.com/cms/shows/rss-import
- toppodcast.com/submit-a-podcast

- tunein.com/podcasters
- womeninpodcasting.com/add-podcast (Only if you have a female host or co-host)

As a bonus, just by submitting your podcast to Apple Podcasts, you'll also show up on all these apps, which draw their podcasts from the Apple directory. You don't even need to do anything!

- Castaway 2
- Castro
- DoggCatcher
- Downcast
- iCatcher
- Overcast
- Podcastland
- Podcruncher
- Pod Link
- RSS Radio

YouTube

An additional option for distributing your podcast is to put it on YouTube.

As I mentioned way back in Chapter 5, using Headliner to create an audiogram of your entire episode would allow you to upload this to YouTube, or you could even create a video yourself, with just a static image and the audio from your podcast, and upload that to YouTube.

There is a lot of debate over whether this is worth your time doing. On the plus side, YouTube is the second biggest search engine in the world. So, if you upload your podcasts there, and use good SEO practices: meta tags; descriptions; and so on (which you can cut and paste directly from your show notes if you wish), then it's another way for people to be able to find your podcast.

Another benefit of YouTube is that literally everyone knows how to use YouTube. Not everyone listens to podcasts, and that isn't necessarily because they're not interested in the content, it's just because they haven't come across podcasts they want to listen to and don't really know how to do it. I can pretty much guarantee that you will talk to people about your podcast and some of them will be too embarrassed to admit that they don't actually know how to listen to one.

But everyone and their grandmother knows how to use YouTube. That means they may start listening to you in a place where they're already comfortable, and then later on decide to seek you out in a podcast app.

There's an opportunity for more interaction on YouTube than you may have in other arenas, because there are likes, dislikes, and comments where people can talk to you directly about what they like or don't like about your show, and you can respond to them directly. While less than 5% of *Fallacious Trump*'s listens come from our YouTube channel, it's probably responsible for more than 25% of our direct feedback.

Another great thing about YouTube is that if you have a transcription of your podcast, you can upload that directly to YouTube as a set of captions, and Google will then index that and give you even better SEO as well as allowing people who are either dDeaf; listening in a noisy environment; or listening in their second language, to be able to follow along by reading the captions.

If you don't want to do either an audiogram or a static image with audio, you could think about filming yourself while recording the podcast. In this way, you could either simply upload the video to YouTube and the audio everywhere else, or you could even make yours a video podcast. Video podcasts are a LOT rarer than audio ones, but some media hosts are able to cope with them just fine.

Some of the remote interview software we talked about in Chapter 4 will also allow you to record video so you could create the video directly with just a webcam, while recording your audio.

You could also use YouTube simply as a promotional tool, where you just post some highlights of your episode (maybe in audiogram form), with links to your website so that people can hear the whole episode.

So, you'll recall that earlier on I said there was debate on whether YouTube was worth it, and then I've given you a lot of benefits but no drawbacks. Well, here's the drawback:

It takes time. Depending on how you choose to use it (such as creating a video podcast), potentially a LOT of time. You really have to decide for yourself whether the benefits you get are worth your time.

For *Fallacious Trump*, I use Headliner to make an audiogram and upload that. I make a quick custom thumbnail in Photoshop and I cut and paste pretty much all the metadata from the ID3 tags I've already written. I've been a YouTuber for more than a decade, so it doesn't take me long to do. We get somewhere around 5% of our total listeners through YouTube, and to be honest many of those don't listen to nearly as much of an episode as our regular listeners do.

For me, since I've streamlined the process so that it doesn't add much to my workflow, I feel it's worth it. You may disagree.

Ultimately, it comes down again to making sure that the work that you choose to do is sustainable. If adding YouTube into the mix makes it too hard for you to keep your quality or consistency going, then it's really not needed.

Analytics

All podcast media hosts will give you some analytics, and if you're anything like me you'll spend an unhealthy amount of time staring at them when you upload a new episode. Watching those numbers go up is kind of addictive sometimes!

It's useful to remember that what they are usually representing is how many people have downloaded your file to their smartphone or computer or tablet, or however they are going to listen to your podcast. In most cases, your media host doesn't know how many people have actually listened to it or how much they listen to.

In most cases, the analytics you get from your podcast host will be quite basic, and often they won't include people listening on Spotify or Spreaker, unless you go through some extra steps to make that happen. The reason for that is that those platforms do not refer people to your RSS feed each time they try to listen to your episode. Instead, when your RSS feed refreshes with a new episode, both Spotify and Spreaker each download a single instance of your podcast, and then host that audio themselves.

However, some hosts now are able to integrate their analytics with Spotify, although I haven't yet seen any which do the same with Spreaker – which is far less important anyway, as it's a much smaller platform.

There are other places, however, that you might want to go to get more data or more specific data. If you go directly to Spotify, then you can get demographic data of the age of your listeners, how many are male, how many female, and so on - but remember, this is only data for Spotify not for any of the other platforms.

Podcastsconnect from Apple Podcasts also has analytic data, and they can tell you more about people actually listening to your podcast rather than just downloading it. They will also give you some 'average consumption' information - that is, how much of an episode people tend to listen to. So, you can look at that data and see which of your episodes were less interesting to people and which were more engaging and got people to listen right to the end. Based on that, you may be able to make decisions about what kind of things to feature in your episodes in the future.

Again, that data is only for people listening through Apple Podcasts, so it won't give you a full picture of all of the people listening to your podcast.

There are three other useful and free services which you can use to find out more information or simply to get information in a single place.

The first is Chartable, which tracks your chart position in the Apple Podcast charts in a variety of countries, and it also tracks all of the reviews that you get through the various versions of Apple Podcasts all around the world. So, if someone in Australia gives you a review. It won't show up when you log into iTunes or Apple Podcasts in the US, but Chartable can tell you about it.

Depending on which podcast media host you're with, you may be able to integrate your host with Chartable, and thereby get additional analytics data. If you look at the media hosting table in Chapter 1, you will see which hosts can integrate with Chartable and which can't.

Another service is called Podtrac. This can be used to get very reliable stats. It's not especially attractive, but it is a good place to go for data, and one analytics element that you get from Podtrac that you don't get from anywhere else is called 'unique monthly audience'. That tells you how many actual people listened to your podcast, during a given month. So, if you make an episode every single week, and your episodes usually get around 500 downloads in the first thirty days, then you will usually average around 2000 downloads per month. But Podtrac will tell you how many people actually listened during that month, which is potentially useful when talking to advertisers, or when trying to figure out roughly how many new listeners you've picked up versus how many subscribers you have (a metric which is frustratingly hard to pin down).

The final service is called Podkite. Similarly to Chartable, this tracks charts and reviews of your podcast, and you can set it to send you an email on a regular basis with your latest chart positions and any reviews that your podcast has been given.

7. Marketing

The launch

It's all very well making a podcast, but it's likely that you want people to actually listen to it. So, rather than just uploading your RSS feed to the various podcast apps, you might need to do a bit of marketing to get people to find out about your podcast.

Many people will be starting from scratch, but if you already have a following in your niche, whether that's a large, engaged social media audience, or an existing email list, it may be worth planning for a specific launch date that you can actively promote in the hope of getting lots of people listening right from the start.

If you have that ability, this is a good practice because the charts on Apple Podcasts, and many other apps, are based on the number of people who subscribe in a particular timeframe. So, if you can get lots of people listening at once, hopefully lots of them will subscribe, which means that you can get some exposure by rising up the charts and being noticed by people for that. If you do really well, you could even make it into the 'New and Noteworthy' section on Apple Podcasts, which has been said to have a significant positive impact on listener numbers.

If you do choose to have a big launch on a specific date, it's a great idea to have more than one episode already uploaded, so that once people have listened to your first episode there's more things for them to listen to. Ideally, everyone will listen and subscribe, and then they will get your subsequent episodes, but it's even better if they can start to form their relationship with your podcast by listening to multiple episodes in one go.

If, however, you don't have the capacity to throw a lot of marketing at a launch date or if you don't have an existing audience, and you're building everything up from nothing, then there's no particular benefit to launching with more than one episode. You may as well simply start podcasting and start telling people about your podcast.

The main thing to remember with your marketing is to be patient; it can take a while to build up an audience. The ideal situation is that the people who listen will subscribe and keep coming back and listening to your subsequent episodes, and each week, each month, you will pick up more new listeners who will also subscribe and gradually your audience will grow and grow.

There's still a number of different things you can do along the way to help make that happen. The first thing is to have a website for your podcast.

Your website

Many podcasts hosts will give you a very basic web page. This is a good thing to start with, but it's great if you have a website that you control, and that you can customise and brand better for your specific podcast.

Why do you need a website for a podcast, why can't people just listen on their podcast apps? Well, some people will listen through the embedded player on your website - that's how you'll get some of your listens.

It's also a hub to send people to. If you tell people to go to Apple Podcasts and listen, then you miss out on all of the people who own who don't have iPhones or iPads. If you tell people to go to Stitcher, then people who don't choose to use that podcast app, probably won't do it.

However, if you send people to your website you can have links to several of the most common sites or apps that people use, and anyone who doesn't want to listen directly on your website can use those to subscribe or find your podcast, using the apps that they're most comfortable with. You don't have to list every app on your site - in fact, doing so would probably be a negative because giving people too many choices can cause confusion and inaction, but linking to the most common ones gives most people an opportunity to subscribe on an app that they like using.

As a hub, it simplifies your life in that there is a single place you can direct anyone to for information about your podcast. You can put it on your social media; you can put it in your email signature; you can mention it on at the end of your episodes; and anytime you need to tell people about your podcast, you can tell people to simply go to your website to find out all about it.

It allows you to have much more detailed show notes than you can have simply using the description box in your ID3 tags, so that you can point people towards all of the things that you mentioned in your show, whether that's news stories, websites or books, and it's pretty much the only way you can embed videos and images. It also your only option if you want to post transcripts of your show, which are great for SEO.

Speaking of SEO, since you'll be updating your site every time that you upload a new episode to your podcast, then it will constantly have new fresh content, which helps your search ranking on Google.

Having a website specifically for your podcast also looks more professional so people will take your podcasts more seriously, and perhaps be more likely to subscribe.

Social media

There are lots of social media options that you can use to promote your podcast, and according to surveys, podcast listeners are even more active on social media than their non-podcast listening friends.

To some extent, how much you can do is again about what you can reasonably achieve. It's unlikely that you will be able to be on every single social media platform, and have a real relationship with the people on that platform - you can't be everywhere at once. I would choose two or three at most, that you can regularly visit and talk to people on and through those, people can find your website and interact with you.

Think about the demographics of your audience, and which networks they are likely to be on. If your show is about business and finance, LinkedIn is probably a good place to talk about it. If your target audience is teenagers, Snapchat, Instagram and maybe even TikTok are more likely to reach them.

Whichever networks you're on, make sure you're not just promoting. Post things that are relevant to your subject, interesting, or add value for your audience. Follow other people, especially people who you might want to invite on your show as guests. Interact with people in a genuine way – be a part of the community. And when you do promote, don't restrict yourself to just your most recent episode – if your old episodes are still relevant and interesting, let people know about them regularly. There will always be people who didn't hear them first time around.

Images and video get far more engagement than simple text posts on platforms like Twitter and Facebook. While podcasting isn't usually a very visual medium, there are ways around that. You can pull a quote from your episode, maybe something intelligent said by a guest in an interview, and create an image out of it. Alternatively, this would be a great place to use one of those audiogram highlights of part of your episode that might make people want to hear more.

On Facebook you can create a specific community. For *Fallacious Trump* we have a closed group, which people join to talk specifically about the show, and about critical thinking and politics. By doing that, we've created a community where everyone feels like they're kind of part of a club. Those people who we talk to regularly become brand ambassadors, and because they like us and they like our show, they go out and tell other people about the show and get other people to listen.

Merchandise

There's almost no limit to the kinds of merchandise you can create for your show. T-shirts, mugs, hats, badges, stickers, and bags are all fairly standard, but there may be something a bit different that is specifically relevant to your podcast that your audience might like. The regular opening voiceover on the *Cognitive Dissonance* podcast ends with the phrase *"There is no welcome mat"*, to indicate the hosts' take-no-prisoners approach to the subjects they discuss. As the show grew in popularity, they kept getting requests for a *Cognitive Dissonance* welcome mat so, for a while at least, they made one that fans could buy.

While an item like that might be a special order, there are many fulfilment services where you can design products for people to buy with no upfront cost. They produce the products on demand, and when someone orders, you get a percentage of the price they pay.

We use TeePublic, but Spreadshirt, Zazzle, Teespring, CafePress and others all provide a similar service with their own ranges of apparel, homeware or promotional items for you to choose from.

You can even give away podcast branded T-shirts, mugs and other items in competitions, or giveaways on your social media pages (do check the rules on your platform of choice first, as some can be quite strict). And then hopefully the winners will spread the word about your podcast when they wear their new T-shirt, which is branded with your podcast logo.

Cross promotion

The podcast industry is very inclusive and helpful to other podcasters, and there are many opportunities for cross promotion with other podcasters - whether that is having them on your show as a guest (and hoping they bring some of their audience with them); or being a guest on other people's shows, which is a great way to get your word out about your podcast, because you're tapping in to a group of people who already listen to podcasts, and if they like what you have to say it's very easy for them to seek out your podcast.

The table at the end of Chapter 3 of places to find guests for your show, is also a good resource for finding podcasts willing to have you on as a guest.

You can also cross promote with other podcasters by creating a thirty or sixty second trailer for your podcast, and getting other podcasters to play your trailer, in exchange for you playing one that promotes their show. Some media hosting companies will help you to get in contact with other podcasters who use their hosting service, and there are various Facebook groups that will help you to connect with podcasters who are looking to cross promote, including the *Podcasters Support Group*, which matches up people looking for cross promotion at the beginning of every month.

Finally, Audry.io is a free community which is designed to help podcasters find each other in order to arrange cross promotions, interviews, collaborations or anything else you can dream up with other podcasters in your niche.

Press

This might not be relevant to everyone, but depending on the topic of your show and if you have something newsworthy to talk about, it may be worth writing a press release and sending it around to relevant publications. For example, if you do a podcast about a particular sport, and there is a magazine that focuses on that sport, their readers might be interested to hear about your show.

The best chance of success with this method is if you have a show which is of interest in a local area. Local newspapers, radio stations and magazines are always on the lookout for stories with a local angle, so it's worth getting in touch to see if they might be interested in featuring you.

If you're podcasting because you have some expertise in a specific subject, you should definitely sign up to a free service called Help A Reporter Out, or HARO. Journalists and bloggers from all over the world – many from major media organisations - post queries every day on topics they're writing about, looking for sources to interview.

Similar opportunities can sometimes be found on Twitter, by following the hashtag #Journorequest, which some journalists use when looking for sources. This is more commonly used in the UK, but some international journos use it as well. Replying to a tweet like this a few years ago got my small business featured in the Sunday Times.

Advertising

If you have some kind of marketing budget, you can also advertise your show, and this can be a good way to get new listeners.

There are some podcast apps which will accept advertising such as Castro, or Overcast, where your text ad appears below the controls on the phone screen when people are already listening to a podcast. This makes it very easy for them to click on that ad, and go directly to your podcast.

It can get quite expensive. Prices on Overcast start at around $110 for a month, and the price varies by genre of podcast, climbing to around $650 per month for more popular genres. Castro has a fixed price of $99 per week, and both services suggest you can pick up anywhere from ten to fifty new subscribers per week.

You could use Facebook or Google ads to advertise your show. The benefit of these, which is especially true of Facebook, is that you can be quite granular in targeting the kinds of people who might be interested in your show. Say, for example, your podcast is about the best new educational toys for young children. You can target your ad specifically to parents with kids from one to five, who have bought kid's toys in the past year, and who already listen to podcasts. By narrowing the scope of who sees your ad, you dramatically increase its effectiveness.

You can even advertise on billboards – yes, physical billboards – using a service called Blip. As with local press, this is especially useful if your podcast is specific to a local area, and in this case it's USA only, but advertising on billboards in that area might give people a reason to seek out your show.

And finally, you can advertise on other podcasts using a service such as Podcorn, which helps smaller podcasters find sponsors. So, you can put an ad up on Podcorn and people will apply to feature your podcast on their show, along with a price. You can choose whose show you think will be relevant to your audience and pay to have them read an ad about how great your podcast is.

8. Monetisation

Podcasting can be an excellent way to promote your business, book, online course, or other money-making venture, but even if you're just doing it for fun, it is possible to make a little money directly through your podcast.

A word of warning, though. It takes time to build up the kind of audience that will be monetizable, and can be a lot of work, so if you're thinking about getting into podcasting as a way to make money, you should probably spend your time doing something else. However, if you look at it as a nice bonus to a hobby you enjoy, or a way to cover hosting fees and the odd bit of new kit, these ideas might help.

Patreon

One of the most common ways that podcasters get support from their audience is using a service such as Patreon, which allows people to pay for content that they enjoy consuming and thereby support the creator. Many artists, musicians, YouTubers, authors and podcasters use systems like this, and while the percentage of people who will voluntarily pay for what is essentially a free piece of entertainment is small, it's not zero.

You can start a Patreon page right from the very beginning of your podcast, and let people know about it so that they can support you if they start to become a fan. You can offer them exclusive content or other benefits to encourage people to sign up, and you can set different tiers so that people can pay a small amount each month, or whatever they can afford.

Over time, Patreon income can build up, but you do have to be very patient, because you won't get lots of patrons immediately, unless you have a very large audience.

While Patreon is the most widely used, it does have a number of competitors, of which the most popular are Glow.fm, Ko-fi, and Buy Me A Coffee. The fees for these services vary. If you want to offer your supporters some benefits, Patreon will take 8%, Glow charges you $0.55 per supporter per month, Ko-fi wants a flat $6 per month and Buy Me A Coffee will cost you 5%. All of them charge standard payment processing fees as well.

Affiliates

As your audience grows, you can start to charge sponsors to be advertised on your show, but for most sponsorship schemes you need a significant number of listeners. The earliest you can reasonably promote products is with an affiliate scheme. With this kind of setup, you only get paid if a customer buys a product or signs up to a service using your special code or website.

While there isn't technically a minimum specific number of audience members in order to be accepted for most affiliate services, obviously the larger your audience is, the more chance you have of making a sale.

Many online stores and service providers have affiliate schemes, and some podcast media hosts will even help you with this. You can sign up to places like ShareASale or CJ Affiliate (which used to be called Commission Junction) and promote products that you think your audience will find useful or interesting.

Lots of large retailers run their own schemes, so think about which products your audience might be interested in. If your podcast is about books then the popular Audible affiliate scheme would be perfect, as there is significant overlap between podcast listeners and audiobook listeners.

If there's something that is specifically relevant to your audience, you might need to check multiple sites. For example, if you make a podcast about video games, there are lots of game retailers to visit online and check to see if they have an affiliate scheme. If nothing is mentioned on their website, you could even contact their offices to find out if they offer something similar.

Sponsorship

We talked about Podcorn in Chapter 7, as an example of places you can advertise your show. It's also currently one of the only places you can find sponsors for your own podcast when your audience is still small.

The types of advertisers who are on Podcorn range from other podcasters, authors, and local businesses up to charities, smartphone apps, and subscription box providers. Generally, they have a smaller budget so they're looking for niche audiences with specific demographics. That's where you come in. Once you sign up, you can apply to do reviews, giveaways, interviews or host-read ads and offer them a price based on the size and demographics of your audience.

When you're looking for sponsors, keep your listeners in mind. Don't waste their time with ads for irrelevant products or services that don't align with your brand or the subject of your show. If you annoy your listeners and they stop listening, then you no longer have a show to sponsor.

Even on Podcorn, the more regular listeners you have, the more chance you will have of getting accepted, and the more money you're likely to make. There is a new site called PodGrid which looks to be trying something similar to Podcorn but as of this writing they are still too new to offer much information. It's probably worth signing up to their email list to get information as it comes out.

Once your listenership gets above 2,500 downloads per episode in the first 30 days, you can start to use some of the other sponsorship options such as ad agencies. That's the cut-off point for signing up to AdvertiseCast, which works with a lot of well-known brands.

Some podcast media hosts will help you to find sponsors once you've shown you can draw a crowd. Whooshkaa say they help their top performing 10% of podcasts to monetise in this way, and Libsyn will help once you hit 5,000 monthly US downloads. Others don't give specific details, but it's a good bet they're looking to help their more successful customers first.

After that, the demands get a little steep. Midroll – one of the best known agencies – won't look at you until you're getting 30,000 downloads per episode in the first 60 days, and Archer Ave don't talk to anyone with less than 50,000 per episode in the first 30 days! Most of us can only dream of ever speaking to Archer Ave. If you make it, don't forget us little guys who helped you along the way!

Starting a Podcast in 2020

Picture Credits

- Pages 11, 25, 28 – Mockup images by Alexandru Circo on dribbble
- Page 34 – Blue Yeti image by Evan-Amos of Vanamo Media
- Page 34 – ATR2100 image by NeONBRAND on Unsplash
- Page 36 – Image by Sven Brandsma on Unsplash
- Page 37 – Image by Oscar Ivan Esquivel Ortega on Unsplash
- Page 38 – Image by Pexels on Pixabay
- Page 39 – Image by Convertkit on Unsplash
- Page 41 – Image by Dmitry Demidov on Pexels
- Pages 43, 44 – Photo by author
- Page 50 – Screenshot used with permission from Envato Market
- Page 53 – Photo by author
- Page 53 – Screenshot used with permission from VB Audio
- Page 63 – Screenshot used under Creative Commons Attribution Licence version 3.0 from Audacity. Audacity® software is copyright © 1999-2020 Audacity Team. The name Audacity® is a registered trademark of Dominic Mazzoni
- Page 63 – Hindenburg screenshot used with permission from Hindenburg
- Page 64 – Reaper screenshot used with permission. Reaper is a registered trademark of Cockos Incorporated
- Page 64 – Adobe product screenshot reprinted with permission from Adobe. ['Adobe', 'After Effects', 'Audition', and 'Premiere', are either registered trademarks or trademarks of Adobe in the United States and/or other countries.
- Page 73 – "Laughing" by AomAm, "Microphone" by abderraouf omara. Both from the Noun Project
- Page 79 – Screenshot used with permission from Auphonic
- Page 86 – Screenshot used with permission from Otter.ai

'Apple', 'Apple Podcasts', 'Mac', 'iTunes', 'iPhone', 'iPad', 'GarageBand', and 'Logic Pro X' are trademarks of Apple Inc., registered in the U.S. and other countries

Index

A

advertising 118
affiliate schemes 122
analytics 106, 107
Apple Podcasts 96, 98, 107
audio clips 52, 53
audio interfaces 36, 37
audiograms 88
Auphonic 79, 80

B

boom arms 39

C

call to action 55
co-host 15, 16, 17
cover art 98, 99
cross promotion 116

D

DAW .... *See* digital audio workstation
digital audio recorders 37
digital audio workstation 62, 63, 64, 65, 66
duration 23, 24, 25

E

editing 62, 63, 64, 65, 66, 74, 90

F

format 20, 21
frequency 25

G

guests 18, 19, 57, 59, 60, 61

H

headphones 38

I

ID3 tags 80, 81
interview 17, 18, 19, 20, 44, 56, 57, 58, 67
intro 48, 49

L

loudness 77, 79

M

marketing 109-119
media hosts 30, 32
merchandise 115
metadata .... *See* ID3 tags
microphones 33, 34, 35, 36, 39, 72
monetisation 120
music 48, 50, 51, 52

N

name 27, 28, 29

O

opening .... *See* intro
outro 22, 55

P

Patreon 120, 121
podcast directories 100, 101, 102
Podcast Mirror 94, 95
pop filters 41
post production 74
press 117

R

remote recording 52, 53, 67, 68, 69

RSS feed 92, 93, 94, 96

S

show notes 83, 84
social media 29, 113
sound treatment 42, 43, 70
sponsorship 123

T

topic 10, 11, 12
transcripts 85, 86, 87

V

voiceover 48, 49, 55
volume .... *See* loudness

W

website 29, 111, 112

Y

YouTube 88, 103, 104, 105

Made in the USA
Coppell, TX
19 November 2020